Susan Neiman

Left Is Not Woke

polity

Copyright © Susan Neiman 2023

The right of Susan Neiman to be identified as Author of this Work has been asserted in accordance with the UK Copyright, Designs and Patents Act 1988.

First published in 2023 by Polity Press

Polity Press
65 Bridge Street
Cambridge CB2 1UR, UK

Polity Press
111 River Street
Hoboken, NJ 07030, USA

All rights reserved. Except for the quotation of short passages for the purpose of criticism and review, no part of this publication may be reproduced, stored in a retrieval system or transmitted, in any form or by any means, electronic, mechanical, photocopying, recording or otherwise, without the prior permission of the publisher.

ISBN-13: 978-1-5095-5830-8

A catalogue record for this book is available from the British Library.

Library of Congress Control Number: 2022948592

Typeset in 11 on 14 pt Sabon by
Cheshire Typesetting Ltd, Cuddington, Cheshire
Printed and bound in the United States by King Printing Co., Inc.

The publisher has used its best endeavors to ensure that the URLs for external websites referred to in this book are correct and active at the time of going to press. However, the publisher has no responsibility for the websites and can make no guarantee that a site will remain live or that the content is or will remain appropriate.

Every effort has been made to trace all copyright holders, but if any have been overlooked the publisher will be pleased to include any necessary credits in any subsequent reprint or edition.

For further information on Polity, visit our website: politybooks.com

Contents

1 Introduction   1
2 Universalism and Tribalism   11
3 Justice and Power   57
4 Progress and Doom   92
5 In Conclusion   127

Acknowledgments   144
Notes   146

1
Introduction

What this book is not: a call for bipartisanship, or a screed against cancel culture. Nor will I speak of the liberal virtue of working to understand those who do not share your views, though I think it's a virtue. But I don't consider myself a liberal, perhaps because I live on a continent where 'liberal' just means 'libertarian,' and a variety of left-wing positions is always on offer. My own allegiances have always been partisan: I was raised in Georgia during the Civil Rights Movement and turned left from there. At a time when even 'liberal' is often a slur in American culture, it's easy to forget that 'socialist' was once a perfectly respectable political position in the land of the free. None other than Albert Einstein wrote a proud defense of socialism at the height of the Cold War. Like Einstein and so many others, I'm happy to be called leftist and socialist.

What distinguishes the left from the liberal is the view that, along with political rights that guarantee freedoms to speak, worship, travel, and vote as we choose, we also have claims to social rights, which undergird the

Introduction

real exercise of political rights. Liberal writers call them benefits, entitlements, or safety nets. All these terms make things like fair labor practices, education, healthcare, and housing appear as matters of charity rather than justice. But these, and other social rights to cultural life, are codified in the United Nation's 1948 "Universal Declaration of Human Rights." While most member states ratified it, no state has yet created a society that assures those rights, and the Declaration has no legal force. In 530 languages it is the world's most translated document, but the Declaration remains aspirational. To stand on the left is to insist that those aspirations are not utopian.

"It is quite possible to move gradually toward participatory socialism by changing the legal, fiscal, and social system in this or that country, without waiting for the unanimity of the planet," writes economist Thomas Piketty.[1] He argues that this can be done via tax increases that would amount to less than the tax rates in the United States and Britain during the post-war period of greatest economic growth. Identity conflicts, he concludes, are fueled by disillusionment with the very ideas of a just economy and social justice.[2] Still this book won't discuss the view that the left should pay more attention to economic than to other inequalities. I think this is true, but that position has been defended before. What concerns me most here are the ways in which contemporary voices considered to be leftist have abandoned the philosophical ideas that are central to any left-wing standpoint: a commitment to universalism over tribalism, a firm distinction between justice and power, and a belief in the possibility of progress. All these ideas are connected.

Introduction

Except as occasional targets, they are hard to find in contemporary discourse. This has led a number of my friends in several countries to conclude, morosely, that they no longer belong to the left. Despite lifetimes of commitment to social justice, they're estranged by developments on what's called the woke left, or the far left, or the radical left. I am unwilling to cede the word 'left,' or accept the binary suggestion that those who aren't woke must be reactionary. Instead, I'll examine how many of today's self-identified left have abandoned core ideas any leftist should hold.

At a moment when anti-democratic nationalist movements are rising on every continent, don't we have more immediate problems than getting the theory right? A left-wing critique of those who seem to share the same values might look like an instance of narcissism. But it's not small differences that separate me from those who are woke. These are not only matters of style or tone; they go to the very heart of what it means to stand on the left. The right may be more dangerous, but today's left has deprived itself of the ideas we need if we hope to resist the lurch to the right.

The lurch is international, and organized. From Bangalore to Budapest and beyond, right-wing nationalists meet regularly to share support and strategies, although each nation thinks its civilization superior. The solidarity between them suggests that nationalist beliefs are only marginally based on the idea that Hungarians/Norwegians/Jews/Germans/Anglo-Saxons/Hindus are the best of all possible tribes. What unites them is the principle of tribalism itself: you will only truly connect with those who belong to your clan, and you need have no deep commitments to anyone else.

Introduction

It's a bitter piece of irony that today's tribalists today find it easier to make common cause than those whose commitments stem from universalism, whether they recognize it or not.

The woke are not a movement in any traditional sense. The first recorded use of the phrase *stay woke* was in the great bluesman Lead Belly's 1938 song "Scottsboro Boys," dedicated to nine black teenagers whose execution for rapes they never committed was only prevented by years of international protests. Staying woke to injustice, being on the watch for signs of discrimination – what could be wrong with that? Yet in a few short years, *woke* was transformed from a term of praise to a term of abuse. What happened?

From Ron DeSantis to Rishi Sunak to Eric Zemmour, *woke* became a battle cry to attack anyone standing against racism, much as the phrase *identity politics* was turned inside out a few years earlier. Yet the right cannot bear all the blame. Barbara Smith, a founding member of the Combahee River Collective, which invented the term, insists that *identity politics* became used in ways that were never intended. "We absolutely did not mean that we would only work with people who are identical to ourselves," she said. "We strongly believed in working with people across various identities on common problems."[3]

Some may argue that the seeds of abuse were present in the original intentions, but it's clear that neither identity nor woke politics was used with the nuance they demanded. Both became divisive, creating alienation that the right quickly exploited. Universities and corporations are more prone to woke excess than community organizers working on the ground. The worst abuses are those of woke capitalism, which hijacks demands for diversity in order to increase profit. Historian Touré Reed argues that the process is calculated: corporations believe that hiring black staff will allow them to tap into black markets.[4] The seizure is often straightforward and unashamed. McKinsey's report on the film industry stated that "By addressing the persistent racial inequities, the industry could reap an additional $10 billion in annual revenues – about 7 percent more than the assessed baseline of $148 billion."[5] But even without raw exploitation of what began as progressive goals, *woke* has become a politics of symbols instead of social change. Woke capitalism was called the dominant motif at Davos 2020, but the gathering welcomed opening speaker Donald Trump with a standing ovation.[6] The fact that rightwing politicians spit out the word *woke* with scorn should not stop us from examining it.

Can *woke* be defined? It begins with concern for marginalized persons, and ends by reducing each to the prism of her marginalization. The idea of intersectionality might have emphasized the ways in which all of us have more than one identity. Instead, it led to focus on those parts of identities that are most marginalized, and multiplies them into a forest of trauma.

Woke emphasizes the ways in which particular groups have been denied justice, and seeks to rectify and repair the damage. In the focus on inequalities of power, the concept of justice is often left by the wayside.

Woke demands that nations and peoples face up to their criminal histories. In the process it often concludes that all history is criminal.

What's confusing about the woke movement is that it expresses traditional left-wing emotions: empathy for the marginalized, indignation at the plight of the oppressed, determination that historical wrongs should be righted. Those emotions, however, are derailed by a range of theoretical assumptions that ultimately undermine them. *Theory* is such a nebulous and trendy concept that it's even been used to launch a fashion line, but if the word today has no clear content, it does have some direction. What unites very different intellectual movements bound together by the word *theory* is a rejection of the epistemological frameworks and political assumptions inherited from the Enlightenment. You need not spend years deciphering Judith Butler or Homi Bhabha to be influenced by theory. We rarely notice the assumptions now embedded in the culture, for they're usually expressed as self-evident truths. Because they are offered as simple descriptions of reality rather than ideas we might question, it's hard to challenge them directly. Those who have learned in college to distrust every claim to truth will hesitate to acknowledge falsehood.

The *New York Times* is a good place to start, since it sets standards in more than one country. While it still embodies the mainstream neoliberal consensus it always represented, since 2019 it has been increasingly, demonstratively woke. In addition to the contested *1619 Project,* that turn has led to real progress, noticeably an increase in the number of black and brown voices and faces. But here's a sentence the paper of record printed in 2021: "Despite Vice President Kamala D. Harris's Indian roots, the Biden administration may prove less forgiving over Modi's Hindu nationalist agenda." If you read that quickly, you may miss the theoretical assumption: political views are determined by ethnic backgrounds. If you know nothing about contemporary

Introduction

India, you may miss the fact that the fiercest critics of Modi's violent Hinducentrism are themselves Indian. The bolder among them call it fascism.

At about the same time, most American media were puzzled by a surprising feature of the 2020 American election. Donald Trump's racism toward blacks and Latinos had been on public display throughout his administration, yet he received more votes from those groups than he had four years earlier. Rather than question, for a moment, the assumption that demography is destiny, journalists hurried to explain the quandary by telling us that Latino communities are diverse: Puerto Ricans are not Cubans, Mexicans are not Venezuelans. Each community has a history, a culture, a set of interests of its own, and deserves to be respected as such. Apart from the fact that this hardly explained the rise in black voters, chopping tribes into tribelets is no solution. *People* are diverse. Neither black nor white nor brown communities are homogenous. We do things for other reasons than being members of a tribe.

Though the presumption that we don't comes from media that are hardly friendly to the current Republican party, the assumptions aren't far from those that drove Donald Trump's practice: appointing a neurosurgeon to head the department of urban development because he was black; giving his feckless son-in-law one of the world's greater foreign policy challenges because he was Jewish; appointing a far-right Catholic to succeed Ruth Bader Ginsberg because both were woman; appointing a diplomatic disaster as ambassador to Germany because he was gay. The fact that Berlin has been a gay-friendly town for most of a century didn't prevent its citizens from undiplomatically expressing shock at Richard

Introduction

Grenell's serial breaches of political conduct. Britain's brief Truss-led government was only the latest to take the same tack: appointing the most diverse cabinet in British history while promoting the most conservative policies in living memory. The fig leaves were too small to cover the shame.

Which do you find more essential: the accidents we are born with, or the principles we consider and uphold? Traditionally it was the right that focused on the first, the left that emphasized the second. That tradition has been turned around when a liberal politician like Hillary Clinton applauds the election of Italy's first female prime minister as a "break with the past," ignoring the fact that Giorgia Meloni's positions are closer to Italy's *fascist* past than those of any of its political leaders since the war. It's not surprising that theories held by the woke undermine their empathetic emotions and emancipatory intentions. Those theories not only have strong reactionary roots; some of their authors were outright Nazis.

How deeply were the intellectual labors of Carl Schmitt and Martin Heidegger connected with their membership in the Nazi party? There's quite a lot of scholarship on the question, and this book will not wade into those weeds. Much of the literature is of the "Yes, but" variety, where 'but' signals the fact that the thinker in question did not accept *every* bit of Nazi ideology, or voiced some quiet criticism, or left the party early. Others offer complex conceptual analyses arguing that some important piece of their thought was incompatible with Nazism. The complexity serves to repress outrage, as if only bad manners, or philosophical shallowness, could give rise to shock. The fact that both men not only

Introduction

served the Nazis, but defended doing so long after the war is old news. Outrage, today, is reserved for racist passages of eighteenth-century philosophy.

However you read the relation between their philosophies and their political commitments, some things are certain: Schmitt rejected universalism and any conception of justice that transcends a notion of power, and Heidegger's anti-modernism and appeals to peasant virtues were more pervasive and deep-rooted than any of his other convictions. These attitudes surely influenced their decisions to throw in their lots with the Nazis – and their refusal to renounce those decisions after the war.

Given the facts, it's puzzling to see the fascination for studying Schmitt by those who are concerned with colonialism, or to hear philosophers concerned with labor rights speak of reading Heidegger against Heidegger. For in fact, many of the theoretical assumptions that support the most admirable impulses of the woke come from the intellectual movement they despise. The best tenets of woke, like the insistence on viewing the world from more than one geographical perspective, come straight from the Enlightenment. But contemporary rejections of the Enlightenment usually go hand in hand without much knowledge of it. This book is written in the hope that philosophy can untangle the confusions that theory has created – and strengthen our political practice in the process. You cannot hope to make progress by sawing at the branch you don't know you are sitting on.

This is not a scholarly book; I'm well aware that many volumes have been written on most of the questions I'll examine. None of my examinations is exhaustive.

Introduction

Scholarly investigation would complicate the claims I make about Foucault or Schmitt or evolutionary psychology. Here I'm less interested in seeking the best possible reading of these and other thinkers than in understanding their influence on contemporary culture. I've no doubt there are readings that would present more generous interpretations of their thought; I have read some of them. Precisely because they are elaborate and counterintuitive, they are not the readings that get a wide hearing. *Isn't good philosophy often elaborate and counterintuitive?* Sometimes. But if you need a Ph.D. and a lot of patience to understand a text – and that in an age where even writers read less – it's hard to imagine that this sort of theoretical work could be as liberating as its intentions. Perhaps the most important thing that distinguishes practitioners of theory from Enlightenment thinkers is that the latter had no intention of writing for a small, select audience; they wrote clearly, without jargon, in the interest of reaching the widest number of readers. (Even Kant, the most difficult of Enlightenment philosophers, wrote fifteen perfectly intelligible essays for a general audience.) I work hard to follow their example.

2
Universalism and Tribalism

Let's begin with the idea of universalism, which once defined the left; international solidarity was its watchword. This was just what distinguished it from the right, which recognized no deep connections, and few real obligations, to anyone outside its own circle. The left demanded that the circle encompass the globe. That was what standing left meant: to care about striking coal miners in Wales, or Republican volunteers in Spain, or freedom fighters in South Africa, whether you came from their tribes or not. What united was not blood but conviction – first and foremost the conviction that behind all the differences of time and space that separate us, human beings are deeply connected in a wealth of ways. To say that histories and geographies affect us is trivial. To say that they determine us is false.

It's certain that shared experiences and histories create particular bonds. We all tend to trust those whose codes we needn't work to crack, whose jokes we get in an instant, whose allusions we recognize immediately. It takes an act of abstraction to become a universalist.

Universalism and Tribalism

Learning languages, and immersing yourself in other cultures, will make that abstraction concrete, but not everyone is as gifted as the great artist and activist Paul Robeson. Yet even without his talents, there are plenty of ways to share, if not to fully enter, other peoples' cultures. You'll never have the same relationship to a culture as do those who fell asleep to its lullabies. But good literature, film, and art can work wonders.

The opposite of universalism is often called 'identitarianism,' but the word is misleading, for it suggests that our identities can be reduced to two dimensions, at most. In fact, all of us have many, whose importance will vary in space and in time throughout our lives. As the philosopher Kwame Anthony Appiah reminds us:

> Until the middle of the twentieth century, no one who was asked about a person's identity would have mentioned race, sex, class, nationality, region or religion.[1]

We are all someone's children, a fact that recedes in importance if we are busy raising our own, but you need only step into your parents' home to shift back to the moment when your primary identity was 'child.' It shifts again when you leave your lover in the morning to take up a professional role at work. Is one of these identities more essential to you than the other? Always? Those shifts of identity are fairly universal, but there are many more. A politically engaged person cannot think of herself as indifferent to politics; a passionate soccer fan cannot envision her identity without loyalty to her home team. Not everyone identifies with whatever they do to make a living, but for those of us who do, imagining ourselves *as ourselves* with an entirely different profession is to imagine a rudderless void.

Universalism and Tribalism

Depending on the person, those components of identity are at least as important as the two that identity politics insists we consider: ethnic and gender identity. A moment's reflection shows even those to be less determinate than supposed. The life of a black person is dramatically different in America and Nigeria, as Chimamanda Adichie so brilliantly showed in *Americanah*. And being Nigerian is only an identifying description outside the country; in a land whose citizens are divided by fraught histories and more than five hundred languages, saying you're Nigerian means nothing at all. Being a Jew in Berlin and a Jew in Brooklyn are experienced so differently that I can assure you they amount to different identities. A Jew in Tel Aviv has another identity again; but a Jew who was born in Tel Aviv has a fundamentally different stance in the world than a Jew who moves there later in life. Is there an Indian identity that holds equally for Hindus and Muslims, Brahmins and Dalits? Can you identify someone as gay without mentioning whether he lives in Tehran or Toledo? The historian Benjamin Zachariah comments:

> Once upon a time, essentializing people was considered offensive, somewhat stupid, anti-liberal, anti-progressive, but now this is only so when it is done by other people. Self-essentializing and self-stereotyping are not only allowed but considered empowering.[2]

Those who condemned essentializing not two decades past are now content to whittle all the elements of our identity down to two. Recent efforts to increase diversity often appeal to the importance of having people in positions of authority who "look like me." It's a remarkably

Universalism and Tribalism

childlike expression, but what do children actually see? People whose heritage is (at least partly) African can have the widest variety of skin tones and hair textures; nor are skin tone or hair texture the only visual qualities we perceive. A child told of someone who "looks like her" might just as well ask: is she taller or shorter? Fatter or thinner? Older or younger? And what about gender?

No one will deny that visual identities are important. When I was a child, people considered attractive in America were not only white but blond. For those of us who weren't, it was a relief when Barbra Streisand entered the limelight, even more when attention turned to Angela Davis. Different as they were, both were beautiful, and neither looked like Marilyn Monroe. The woke movement has made us aware that *white* was not considered to be an identity at all but something between norm and neutrality, as crayons labelled *flesh-colored* suggested that all flesh was pasty pink. Diversity is a good. It just isn't the only one. I'm not the first to point out that diversifying power structures without asking what the power is used for can simply lead to stronger systems of oppression. Nor does it stop with conservative governments appointing the formerly marginalized. At Ian Malcolm's suggestion, Canadian comedian Ryan Long interviewed a variety of bystanders on the question of whether offshore interrogators, which is CIA-speak for torturers, should become more diverse. The fact that he was taken seriously is not funny at all.[3]

The reduction of the multiple identities we all possess to race and gender only appears to be a question of looks. The focus on two dimensions of human experi-

Universalism and Tribalism

ence is a focus on those dimensions that experienced the most trauma. Identity politics embodies a major shift that began in the mid twentieth century: the subject of history was no longer the hero but the victim.[4] Two world wars had undermined the urge to valorize traditional forms of heroism. The impulse to shift our focus to the victims of history began as an act of justice. History had been the story of the victors, while the victims' voices went unheard. This condemned the victims to a double death: once in the flesh, once again in memory. To turn the tables and insist that the victims' stories enter the narrative was just a part of righting old wrongs. If victims' stories have claims on our attention, they have claims on our sympathies and systems of justice. When slaves began to write their memoirs, they took steps toward subjectivity and won recognition – and slowly but certainly, recognition's rewards.

So the movement to recognize the victims of slaughter and slavery began with the best of intentions. It recognized that might and right often fail to coincide, that very bad things happen to all sorts of people, and that even when we cannot change that we are bound to record it. As an alternative to preceding millennia, when the survivor of a massacre by Roman legions or Mongol invaders could expect no more than a laconic "shit happens," this was a step toward progress. Yet something went wrong when we rewrote the place of the victim; the impulse that began in generosity turned downright perverse. The limiting case of this trend is the story of Benjamin Wilkomirski, the Swiss man whose claims to have spent his childhood in a concentration camp turned out to be invented. Earlier rogues sought to hide troubled origins, inventing aristocratic genealogies as a

Universalism and Tribalism

way to climb. Anyone, after all, might be the son of an errant knight or a wayward pope. Now that cachet has given way to another: claiming a more miserable birth than your true one guarantees new forms of status.

Wilkomirski was hardly alone. To escape racist discrimination, light-skinned African Americans once passed as white, leaving families behind to live freer if sadder lives in the dominant class. Recently, however, several white Americans have lost jobs they gained by falsely passing as black. An African American actor was jailed for staging a racist attack on himself.[5] A Jewish German pop star provoked attention and outrage by inventing an antisemitic incident hundreds of hours of police investigations could not confirm.[6] Orchestrated victimhood is perfidious because it mocks the victims of real racist attacks, but I'm less interested now in the consequences than in the fact that they're possible at all. *What was recently a stigma has become a source of standing.* Where painful origins and persecution were once acknowledged, as in Frederick Douglass's narratives, the pain was a prelude to overcoming it. Prevailing over victimhood, as Douglass did, could be a source of pride; victimhood itself was not. The rash of contemporaries inventing worse histories than they experienced is something new.

Fraudulent claims to status are nothing special; just think how many embellish war experiences to center themselves in heroic light. But even without imposters, the valorization of the victim raises problems. What's been dubbed the victimhood Olympics has reached international dimensions. The injunction to remember was once a call to remember heroic deeds and ideals; now *Never Forget!* is a demand to recall suffering. Yet undergoing suffering isn't a virtue it all, and it rarely creates any. Victimhood should be a source of legitimation for claims to restitution, but once we begin to view victimhood *per se* as the currency of recognition, we are on the road to divorcing recognition, and legitimacy, from virtue altogether.

It's a sign of moral progress that we no longer dismiss victims' stories, as we did for so long; they deserve our empathy and, wherever possible, reparations. (It's less a sign of progress, though it may be inevitable, that we have moved from thoughtless dismissal to thoughtless acceptance.) My question is rather what we mean when we call for recognition. Jean Améry did not even want to erect a monument to the victims of the Third Reich because, as he wrote, "to be a victim alone is not an honor."[7] That claim sprang from an assumption that now seems old-fashioned: monuments should be reserved for those whose deeds we admire, whose paths we hope to follow.

Jean Améry was born in 1912 as Hans Mayer, an assimilated Austrian Jew. Too poor to attend university, he became one of the more erudite philosophical writers of his day. Améry fled Vienna for Belgium after the *Anschluß* and joined a resistance group in Brussels, where he was arrested and tortured by the Gestapo, who sent him to Auschwitz on discovering he was a Jew. His book *At the Mind's Limits* may be the most searing confrontation with the Holocaust ever written. There he wrote:

> We did not become wiser in Auschwitz, if by wisdom one understands positive knowledge of the world. We perceived nothing there that we would not already have been

Universalism and Tribalism

> able to perceive on the outside; not a bit of it brought us practical guidance. In the camp too, we did not become deeper, if that calamitous depth is at all a definable intellectual quality. It goes without saying, I believe, that in Auschwitz we did not become better, more human, more humane, and more mature ethically. You do not observe dehumanized man committing his deeds and misdeeds without having all of your notions of inherent human dignity placed in doubt. We emerged from the camp stripped, robbed, emptied out, disoriented – and it was a long time before we were able even to learn the ordinary language of freedom. (ibid.)

Améry wrote admiringly of Frantz Fanon, whose *Black Skin, White Masks* proclaims:
"I am not the slave of the Slavery that dehumanized my ancestors" [emphasis added]. More recently, the philosopher Olúfémi O. Táíwò has argued that

> ... pain, whether born of oppression or not, is a poor teacher. Suffering is partial, shortsighted, and self-absorbed. We shouldn't have a politics that expects different. Oppression is not a prep school.[8]

Táíwò argues that trauma, at best, is an experience of vulnerability that provides a connection to most of the people on the planet, but "it is not what gives me a special right to speak, to evaluate, or decide for a group." (ibid.) He argues that the valorization of trauma leads to a politics of self-expression rather than social change.

Améry and Táíwò's critiques contest important claims of standpoint epistemology, which emphasize the ways our social positions affect our claims to knowledge. As philosopher Miranda Fricker argues:

Universalism and Tribalism

Feminists have taken from Marxism the intuitive idea that a life led at the sharp end of any given set of power relations provides for critical understanding (of the social world, in the first instance) where a life cushioned by the possession of power does not.[9]

Few would dispute this insight, as intuitive as it is important, but two questions remain. Critical understanding *can* arise from powerlessness, but does it always do so? Few champions of standpoint epistemology would argue that it does. And, if not, can we allow the experience of powerlessness to be elevated to an *inevitable* source of political authority?

I'd prefer we return to a model in which your claims to authority are focused on what you've done to the world, not what the world did to you. This wouldn't return the victims to the ash-heap of history. It allows us to honor caring for victims as a virtue without suggesting that being a victim is one as well. Defending convicted murderers facing execution, Bryan Stevenson, founder of the Equal Justice Initiative, argues that everyone is more than the worst thing they ever did. Do you want to be reduced to the worst thing that ever happened to you?

Those on the left who are uncomfortable with universalism should consider: there is no more successful example of identity politics, complete with the appeal to past victimhood, than the Jewish nationalism of Israeli politicians like Binyamin Netanyahu.[10] Identity politics not only contract the multiple components of our identities to one: they essentialize that component over which we have the least control. And though it still refers to a recognizable problem, the words *identity politics* have turned toxic, taken up by conservatives unaware that they are practicing identity politics of their own. I prefer the word 'tribalism,' which beckons barbarity, despite the critique of a well-meaning colleague who expressed concern that the word might be offensive to Native Americans. But the idea wasn't invented in the Americas; it's as old as the Hebrew Bible. The Bible warns us, again and again, about what happens when people unite around tribal identities: envy, strife, and war are the usual consequences. Tribalism is a description of the civil breakdown that occurs when people, of whatever kind, see the fundamental human difference as that between *our kind* and everyone else.

Tribalism is even more paradoxical today, since we know that the idea of race was created by racists.[11] Through most of the nineteenth century, neither the Jews nor the Irish counted as white. Concepts need not be biological in order to have meaning; social constructs are just as real as social conditions like racism make them. But given the history of racial categorization, there is no guarantee that the distinctions we recognize today will have the same meaning for those coming of age in 2050.

The late American sociologist Todd Gitlin's *Letters to a Young Activist* begins by acknowledging the pull of basing politics on tribal identities: "Your starting point is that your identity has been singled out for victimhood. You didn't choose it, but you refuse to walk away from it." But the primordial passion that fuels identity politics proves to be its weakness: "However often it makes the blood race, [identity politics] often enough glosses over a profound impotence." For, he argues, identity politics confuses grand passions with minor irritations, while mocking broader goals as mere rhetoric.

Universalism and Tribalism

On this view, the goal of politics is to make sure your category is represented in power, and the proper critique of other people's politics is that they represent a category that is not yours ... Even when it takes on a radical temper, identity politics is interest-group politics. It aims to change the distribution of benefits, not the rules under which distribution takes place.

Ultimately, Gitlin concludes, identity politics point backward, anchoring us in the past.

Nazi jurists who developed the legal theory behind the infamous Nuremberg Laws studied American race laws. They concluded that the American "one drop of blood" rule would be too harsh to apply in Germany and settled for softer criteria of what counted as Jewish; anyone with no more than one Jewish grandparent could retain German citizenship, however precariously. The jurists appreciated, however, the ways in which American legal realism "demonstrated that it was perfectly possible to have racist legislation even if it was technically infeasible to come up with a scientific definition of race."[12] Still the "one drop of blood" rule underwrote American laws against racial intermarriage and created categories like 'quadroon' and 'octoroon.' When progressive American pundits claim that the Republican Party is doomed to disappear as the white population shrinks, they fall prey to the same shaky thinking that fuels racist fires. Even those who know about social construction persist in giving those categories more power than they deserve; indeed, the more the consensus grows that racial categories have no place in science, the more tenaciously they play a role in political culture.

Universalism and Tribalism

No one denies that your life will be different, and probably shorter, if you were born in Mombasa rather than Manhattan. So, what's universal to humanity that is not a sanctimonious lie? Start with pain. Even in a world saturated with violent images you shudder, for a moment, when you face a photo of a bomb-torn body. Though it's beamed from a foreign country, it could have been your own. You do not make a complicated inference from another's pain to your own; the empathy is instant, though it's usually fleeting. It's the kind of compassion that Jean-Jacques Rousseau argued is prior to reason, and found not just in humans but in many other animals.

And speaking of bodies: they're composed of many parts. Flesh comes in a dizzying array of shapes and colors and sizes, just as cultures and histories do, and it's as interesting as cultures and histories are. But the bones are the framework that holds bodies together. Being a universalist allows you to find fascination and joy in all the ways that people differ – and still come back, time and again, to the bones that build and bind us.

What other common human dispositions can we find across times and places? There's no shortage of candidates, but let's consider another that Rousseau thought was basic, though it's less visceral than sympathy for physical pain. We are born free, and inclined to resist attempts to restrict our freedom, – as recent protests from Hong Kong to Moscow suggest. Moreover, we view it as natural that anyone should resist such attempts. "The declaration that 'we too are human beings,'" wrote Jean-Paul Sartre, "is at the bottom of every revolution."[13] One can go further: every argument against slavery, colonialism, racism, or sexism is

Universalism and Tribalism

embodied in the question "Is she not a human being?" The philosopher Ato Sekyi-Otu says the question is as much at home in his native Akan as it is in Thomas Jefferson's English. Sekyi-Oto thinks it's insulting to suggest the idea of the human had to be imported from Europe.[14]

Judith Butler's question was meant to be rhetorical: "What kind of cultural imposition is it to claim that a Kantian may be found in every culture?" Sekyi-Oto's reply to Butler: "It's no imposition at all; our native vernaculars regularly do that work." (ibid.) Drawing on the best insights of ordinary language philosophy, he urges us to pay attention to what native speakers do when they justify a moral claim. "Give Europe credit," he continues

> ... for giving formal and institutional expression to the common intuitions and dreams of humanity. But do not award the West exclusive proprietary rights. (ibid.)

Appealing to the humanity of those who are being dehumanized is the universal form we use to respond to oppression everywhere. That Jefferson and Kant did not practice what they preached is no argument against the sermon.

Universalism is under fire on the left because it's conflated with fake universalism: the attempt to impose certain cultures on others in the name of an abstract humanity that turns out to reflect just a dominant culture's time, place, and interests. That happens daily in the name of corporate globalism, which seeks to convince us that the key to human happiness is a vast universal mall. But let's stop to consider what a feat it was to make that original abstraction to humanity.

Universalism and Tribalism

Earlier assumptions were inherently particular, as earlier ideas of law were religious, down to the tiny Greek states whose goddesses provided refuge to people who were hounded by the goddesses of the city-state next door. (Consider the *Oresteia*.) Most religious laws had some provision for members of a different religion, albeit most often honored in the breach. But the idea that one law should apply to Protestants and Catholics, Jews and Muslims, lords and peasants, simply in virtue of their common humanity is a recent achievement, which now shapes our assumptions so thoroughly we fail to recognize it as an achievement at all. We should honor that feat of abstraction, even by those Enlightenment thinkers who were unable to scale the towering achievement they'd wrought and got stuck on the rungs of local prejudice.

Let's also consider the opposite: views like those of the Nazi legal theorist Carl Schmitt, who wrote that "anyone who says the word 'humanity' wants to deceive you."[15] Like many of his claims, this one was not original. He was echoing the right-wing thinker Joseph de Maistre, who wrote in 1797:

> Now, there is no such thing as 'man' in this world. In my life I have seen Frenchmen, Italians, Russians, and so on. I even know, thanks to Montesquieu, that one can be Persian. But as for man, I declare I've never encountered him.[16]

Schmitt is considerably more complicated, but rather more appalling. For Schmitt, not even all members of *Homo sapiens* are considered human. His book *Land and Sea* restricts humanity to those who are rooted in the earth. Britons and Fiji Islanders are sea peoples, whom he sometimes calls fish people. (Yes, *Fischmenschen*.) Without a navy or a homeland, Jews are neither fish nor fowl but according to this 1942 text, they are certainly not human. Indeed, Schmitt suggests that universalist concepts like *humanity* are Jewish inventions meant to disguise particular Jewish interests seeking power in a non-Jewish society.[17] The argument is perilously close to the contemporary argument that Enlightenment universalism disguises particular European interests seeking power in an increasingly non-white world.

Neither Counter-Enlightenment critic recognized that *human* is not an empirical concept, the sort of thing like *dog*, or even *Frenchman*, that you can pick out after a moment or two of examining them. Rather than echoing Schmitt's famous quote you might say "Whoever says 'humanity' is making a normative claim." It may be concealed by language like the first sentence of the German constitution: "The dignity of the human is inviolable." As a statement of fact, this is ridiculous; the words were written just a few years after the Third Reich had violated human dignity in hitherto unimaginable ways. What they mean is rather imperative: to recognize someone as human is to acknowledge a dignity in them that *should* be honored. It also implies that this recognition is an achievement: to see humanity in all the weird and beautiful ways it appears is a feat that demands you go beyond appearances. In this sense Foucault was right to say that the human is a recent invention. Like other products of the modern, it was not one he valued, and he expected it to disappear. "Our task," he wrote, "is to emancipate ourselves from humanism" – which requires accepting the death of the human, as he prophesied in his early *The Order of Things*.

Universalism and Tribalism

The abstraction to humanity is precarious, easier to think than to act on. If recognizing someone's humanity means recognizing her right to be treated with dignity, enslaving or annihilating her denies her humanity. Think of blacks treated as beasts of burden or Jews treated as vermin. During the war in Vietnam it was common to hear American commentators solemnly explain that Asians cared less about dying than other peoples. I still remember the newsmen's straight faces.

The left-wing turn to tribalism is particularly tragic because the early civil rights and anti-colonialist movements resolutely opposed tribal thinking in all its forms. Their strengths were expressed in songs that claimed: "All men are slaves till their brothers are free." Tribalism is a dangerous game, as the right realized very early. If the demands of minorities are not seen as human rights but as the rights of particular groups, what prevents a majority from insisting on its own? That question was impossible to overlook after Trump's election as well as in the identitarian movements that have recently grown in England and France, Holland and Germany. Their members consciously present themselves as part of a harmless trend: if other groups are allowed to fight for their rights, why shouldn't white Europeans stand up for theirs?

The answer is not, in fact, very difficult. Shortly after Trump was elected in 2016, a debate broke out in the U.S.: was liberal support for identity politics to blame for the results?[18] Did minor issues about subtle forms of discrimination alienate white voters, who went on to support Trump for more fundamental, economic reasons? The question is misleading. The anti-black racism

Universalism and Tribalism

which often leads to murder is not a minor issue but a crime, as is violence against women and members of LGBT communities. But for those who believe that only tribal interests are genuine, calls for universal outrage in the face of such crimes make no sense; only arguments based on the interests of particular groups will seem like solid ground.

Hannah Arendt thought that Adolf Eichmann should have been tried for crimes against humanity, not for crimes against the Jewish people. It's a distinction that seemed trivial at the time, but its importance is increasingly clear. My support for Black Lives Matter springs neither from tribal membership nor from guilt about wrongs committed by my ancestors, impoverished Eastern European Jews who immigrated to Chicago in the early twentieth century. I support BLM because the killing of unarmed people is a crime against humanity. At the same time, I reject the white countermovement whose members shout "All lives matter," because it uses a banal general truth to distract attention from an important empirical truth, namely, that African Americans are more likely to be subject to violence than other Americans. It's an empirical fact, but you need a concept of truth to see it.

Initially, Black Lives Matter was a universalist movement. Whether measured by numbers of demonstrators (some 26 million in the U.S. alone), or numbers of largely peaceful demonstrations (in some 4,446 American towns), it was the largest social movement in U.S. history. The 2020 demonstrations were more racially diverse than any previous movement against racism. According to research conducted in Los Angeles, New York City, and Washington, D.C., 54 percent of demonstrators identified as white. More than half said it was the first demonstration they had ever attended.

That American rejection of white supremacism reverberated around the world. Not least because Great Britain outsourced most of its slavery to the colonies, the British have been even slower than Americans to remember the histories they'd rather forget. A *Guardian* poll taken three months before the 2020 Black Lives Matter demonstrations showed that merely 19 percent of all Britains felt shame or regret for the British Empire. Hence the speed of change of attitude in Britain was particularly astonishing. The statue of a major slave trader was ceremoniously dumped in the Bristol harbor, the pedestal of Churchill's memorial was sprayed with a reminder of his racism. Symbolic changes have been matched by demands for systemic ones: to make black and colonial history mandatory throughout the school system, to examine police practices which, though not as often deadly in London as they are in New York, are racist nonetheless. Lloyd's of London and other corporations announced reparations for slavery. Statues of King Leopold II, whose policies led to the murder of some ten million Congolese, were splashed with blood-colored paint in Belgium, while other statues the world over are being contextualized. Australians began to offer more than apologies for injustices done to First Peoples. Listening to voices around the world, extraordinarily diverse in age, class, and ethnic background, two things were clear: their well-informed solidarity with the Black Lives Matter movement in America, and their commitments to facing their own racist histories. In Germany, preoccupied for decades with its crimes against the Jews, calls to acknowledge its short but brutal colonial history and return plundered artworks were finally heard. In Japan, far more reluctant to acknowledge its war crimes than its onetime ally, thousands demonstrated for a month in sympathy with black Americans and in protest against ongoing Japanese racism.

None of the protests succeeded in ending police violence, for the problems, we have learned, are structural. As the retired police chief of a major southern city explained to me, the hours of training required to join the police force in his state are fewer than those required to become a hairdresser. You read that right. In some states it is harder to get a license to wash, cut, and dry someone's hair than it is to get a license to enforce the law with a lethal weapon. Information like this suggests that slogans like "Defund the police" are misguided. What's needed is better funding: for police training to learn to distinguish problems of crime and problems of mental health, to care for those whose mental health crises may be misinterpreted as criminal; for community programs that provide skills, training, and hope for young people of color whose otherwise hopeless prospects make rage, or at least drug peddling, the most reasonable of available options.

It's no wonder the protests began in America. This is not just because, though racism is an international problem, more people die of it on the streets of America. (Or in their beds. Breonna Taylor, a young African-American medical worker, was killed in an illegal midnight police raid on her apartment in Louisville, Kentucky.) Even more importantly, unlike other nations, America claims to be founded on a set of ideals. Historians have long worked to show how far American realities diverged from American ideals. But the way from archives to public consciousness is a long one. American exceptionalism still looms large in public understanding of history. While it may acknowledge that American history diverged from its ideals, it focuses attention on attempts to bring them together. Occasionally, even philosophers did so: think of Ralph Waldo Emerson's and Henry David Thoreau's support not only of the quieter sorts of abolitionist, but their ringing defense of John Brown, or William James's denunciation of burgeoning American imperialism. Significantly, African Americans have always played a major role in holding the nation's feet to the fire. Very few supported Back-to-Africa movements. From Frederick Douglass to Paul Robeson to Toni Morrison, African Americans have been at the forefront of those who demand that America live up to the ideals it proclaims. The shock that foreign observers expressed after the 2021 attack on the U.S. Capitol showed that Americans aren't the only ones who cling to those ideals. Friends from Senegal, Egypt, and India called me to express sorrow: they knew that such things happened in their countries, but though they know a great deal about its failures, they still somehow thought that America was different.

Yet despite the universalist character of the 2020 movement, a racist right was quick to dismiss it as a case of identity politics. Perhaps the very breadth and diversity of those demanding an end to violence against black people made them nervous. In June 2020, 77 percent of all Americans agreed that systematic racism is a major problem. When did we ever see polls like that? Alas, it wasn't only the right that moved toward tribal rhetoric. By the Fall of that year few voices speaking in defense of Black Lives Matter were universalist. Some explicitly rejected the idea that it was a movement on behalf of common ideals, though it allowed that white allies could play a role.

I am not an ally. Convictions play a minor role in alliances, which is why they are often short. If my self-interest happens to align with yours, for a moment, we could form an alliance. The United States and the Soviet Union were allies until the Nazi regime was defeated. When the U.S. decided its interests lay in recruiting former Nazis to defeat communism, the Soviet Union turned from ally to enemy. What interest led millions of white people into plague-threatened streets to shout "Black Lives Matter"? This was no alliance, but a commitment to universal justice. To divide members of a movement into allies and others undermines the bases of deep solidarity, and destroys what standing left means.

Of course it isn't just bad theory that feeds the urge to tribalism. Rage plays a role. It is almost unbearable that the largest social movement in American history failed to prevent the continuing murder of people of color. With that knowledge, it must be easy to think that white cops taking a knee in New Jersey or white vets in BLM T-shirts facing down troopers in Oregon counted for nothing.

But they count for something, especially for those of us, black and white, who remember men like Bull Connor. They would count even more if we resist the roots of tribalism. To do that, we need some intellectual history.

It's now an article of faith that universalism, like other Enlightenment ideas, is a sham that was invented to disguise Eurocentric views that supported colonialism.

Universalism and Tribalism

When I first heard such claims some fifteen years ago, I thought they were so flimsy they'd soon disappear. For the claims are not simply ungrounded: they turn Enlightenment upside down. Enlightenment thinkers *invented* the critique of Eurocentrism and were the first to attack colonialism, on the basis of universalist ideas. To see this, you don't need the more difficult texts of the Enlightenment; a paperback edition of *Candide* is enough. For a succinct diatribe against fanaticism, slavery, colonial plunder, and other European evils, you can hardly do better.

My ability to predict intellectual trends turned out to be scant: in the last few years the Enlightenment has been held responsible for most of our misery, just as a century ago, the source for contemporary suffering was called modernity. Something big, after all, must be to blame. Enlightenment-bashing may have begun in American universities, but its reach has swept through the culture in much of the Western world. One of many examples: Germany normally pours millions into national celebrations of its cultural treasures; in the last two decades we've had an Einstein-Jahr, a Luther-Jahr (Luther's virulent antisemitism notwithstanding), a Beethoven-Jahr, a Marx-Jahr. The consensus against Enlightenment is now so broad that it was extremely difficult to organize a year devoted to the 300th birthday of Immanuel Kant.

Enlightenment is a contested concept which means different things even to those of us who study the subject. Its high point in the eighteenth century had predecessors, but here I use the word to refer to an intellectual and political movement that came to flower in 1698 with the publication of Pierre Bayle's *Historical*

Universalism and Tribalism

and Critical Dictionary and ended in 1804 with the death of Kant. The Enlightenment was committed to a number of ideas, but the focus here will be on those I've called fundamental for the left: commitments to universalism, justice, and the possibility of progress. It's clear the Enlightenment did not realize all the ideals it championed, but that's what ideals are about. Some of the criticisms voiced today could have strengthened Enlightenment by showing that, through the restless self-critique it invented, it had the power to right most of its own wrongs. Instead, those who might have realized the Enlightenment have been engaged in attacking it.

They forget that the Enlightenment emerged from a blasted landscape, on a continent soaked with blood. Those who dismiss Enlightenment thinkers as naive or optimistic not only ignore their writings; more importantly, they ignore the history that formed the background to their thought. It was a history of waves of plague without cure, and ever-returning religious wars in which countless people died. (Daniel Kehlmann's best-selling novel *Tyll* provides a vivid picture of that world.) Women were regularly burned alive as suspected witches, men thrown chained into dungeons for writing a pamphlet. From across the Atlantic came news of barbarities visited on the peoples of the New World. Small wonder that no era in history wrote more, or more passionately, about the problem of evil.

Into this landscape the Enlightenment introduced the very idea of *humanity* that its critics, like de Maistre, were unable to recognize. Enlightenment thinkers insisted that everyone, whether Christian or Confucian, Parisian or Persian, is endowed with innate dignity that

33

Universalism and Tribalism

demands respect. Versions of that idea can be found in Jewish, Christian, and Muslim texts that claim at least some of us were made in God's image, but the Enlightenment based it on reason not revelation. Whatever you think happened in the Garden of Eden, you can find your way to this.

From the idea that all people, wherever they come from, have a claim to human dignity, it hardly follows that differences between people do not matter. Individual histories and cultures put flesh on the bones of abstract humanity. What does follow is a notion of human rights that should be guaranteed to everyone, regardless of the history they've lived or the culture they inhabit.

The concept of human rights and its implications for practice have been contested since Jeremy Bentham called them nonsense on stilts in 1796. Yet even without an ontological account of what those rights are, it's clear that the expansion of human rights plays an increasingly significant political role. The writer Tom Keenan argues that rights,

> especially human rights, are better treated as *things we claim* rather than *things we have*. This may seem like a minor matter of words but I believe that it has the potential to challenge profoundly the ways we think about and act with the discourse of human rights. It does not weaken the force of these claims to admit that they are only, or just that, claims; in fact it might make them stronger by making them less essentialist, dogmatic, sacred or as Michael Ignatieff once put it, idolatrous.[19]

To claim that someone's rights have been violated is to understand her suffering as an injustice, not simply

34

a matter for pity. Following Lynn Hunt's now classic *Inventing Human Rights*, Keenan argues that the apparently crippling abstraction of human rights and their lack of metaphysical grounding is a source of their power. "The notion of the 'rights of man,' like the revolution itself, opened up an unpredictable discussion for conflict and change."

So it's not surprising that the attempt to fix a canon of human rights in the wake of World War II's devastation was controversial. The United States recognized political but not social rights. The Soviet Union did not recognize a right to freedom of travel. South Africa wanted nothing that would limit apartheid, Saudi Arabia objected to granting equal rights to women. What's more surprising is that after two years of discussion between committee members from nations as diverse as Canada, Lebanon, and China, a document that aimed to transcend cultural and political differences could be signed at all. With ten abstentions, the fifty-eight nations that belonged to the United Nations at the time agreed to the thirty articles that make up the Universal Declaration of Human Rights. Eleanor Roosevelt, who chaired the committee, knew it could create no binding obligations, but hoped it would "serve as a common standard of achievement for all people of all nations."[20] To be on the left is to uphold that standard, agreeing with the United Nations that

> All human rights are indivisible, whether they are civil and political rights, such as the right to life, equality before the law and freedom of expression; economic, social, and cultural rights, such as the right to work, social security, and education, or collective rights, such as the rights to

development and self-determination, are indivisible, interrelated, and interdependent. The improvement of one right facilitates the advancement of the others. Likewise, the deprivation of one right adversely affects the others.[21]

There are few charges more bewildering than the claim that the Enlightenment was Eurocentric. Perhaps those who make it confuse eighteenth-century realities with the Enlightenment thinkers who fought to change them – often at considerable personal risk. When contemporary postcolonial theorists rightly insist that we learn to view the world from the perspective of non-Europeans, they're echoing a tradition that goes back to Montesquieu, who used fictional Persians to criticize European mores in ways he could not have safely done as a Frenchman writing in his own voice. Montesquieu's *The Persian Letters* was followed by scores of other writings using the same device. Lahontan's *Dialogue with a Huron* and Diderot's *Supplement to Bougainville's Voyage* criticized the patriarchal sexual laws of Europe, which criminalized women who bore children out of wedlock, from the perspective of the more egalitarian Hurons and Tahitians. Voltaire's sharpest attacks on Christianity were written in the voices of a Chinese emperor, and an indigenous South American priest.

In their recent best-seller *The Dawn of Everything*, anthropologist David Graeber and archaeologist David Wengrow make a fascinating argument. Enlightenment critiques of Europe from the perspectives of non-European observers have usually been read as literary strategies: those writers put their own thoughts in the mouths of imagined non-Europeans in order to avoid the persecution they would otherwise face for voicing them. Graeber and Wengrow argue that the non-European interlocuters were real. Their arguments largely rest on a study of Lahontan's *Dialogue with a Huron,* published at the dawn of the Enlightenment in 1703, an enormously successful book that inspired many imitations. The French writer's book recounts a series of conversations with a Wendat thinker and statesman named Kandiaronk, over the course of years Lahontan spent in Canada becoming fluent in Algonquin and Wendat. Instead of assuming, as many had, that indigenous people were incapable of the sophisticated political arguments attributed to Kandiaronk, Graeber and Wengrow present evidence that the historical Kandiaronk was known for his brilliance and eloquence, and engaged in just the sort of debates with Europeans that Lahontan recorded.

Their evidence is inconclusive, and some of their theses about the Enlightenment are questionable. Even if Graeber and Wengrow are right about the influence of the historical Kandiaronk, he was only one example of many indigenous voices that reached Enlightenment ears. Indigenous critiques of money, property rights, and social hierarchies had attracted European attention since the sixteenth century. They surely influenced Enlightenment critiques; we may never know how many of the latter were imagined and how many were not. Like most literary endeavors, they were probably mixtures of both. What the debates over *The Dawn of Everything* underline beyond doubt, however, is that the Enlightenment was pathbreaking in rejecting Eurocentrism and urging Europeans to examine themselves from the perspective of the rest of the world.

Enlightenment discussion of the non-European world was rarely disinterested. Its thinkers studied Islam in order to find another universal religion that could highlight Christian faults. Bayle and Voltaire argued that Islam was less cruel and bloody than Christianity because it was more tolerant and rational. The Sinophilia that swept the early Enlightenment was not just a matter of curiosity about a distant ancient culture; studying the Chinese was part of an agenda. Bourgeois Frenchmen chafing under the feudal restrictions that gave government contracts to the aristocracy praised the Confucian system, where advancement was based on as much merit as national exams can measure. The practice of using bits of cross-cultural anthropology to bolster one's arguments was so common it was used, or parodied, by the Marquis de Sade. Sade provided a twist on a trope: most often, the point of examining non-European cultures was to point out the defects of European ones. In Sade's work, lists of non-European crimes, often accompanied by specious footnotes, are meant to prove the opposite: you will find endless cruelty wherever you go.[22]

Some Enlightenment portraits of non-Europeans will grate on our ears. Given the limited possibilities for travel, eighteenth-century thinkers had to rely on a small number of reports that often repeated caricatures which served colonial interests. But unlike today's critics, Enlightenment thinkers were keenly aware of the gaps in their own knowledge. Here is Rousseau, writing in 1754:

> Although the inhabitants of Europe have for the past three or four hundred years overrun the other parts of the

Universalism and Tribalism

world and are constantly publishing new collections of travels and reports, I am convinced that the only men we know are Europeans ... we do not know the Peoples of the East Indies, who are exclusively visited by Europeans more interested in filling their purses than their heads. All of Africa and its numerous inhabitants, as remarkable in character as they are in color, still remain to be studied; the whole earth is covered with Nations of which we know only the names, and yet we pretend to judge mankind![23]

Rousseau was no exception. Diderot warned against making judgments about China without a thorough knowledge of its language and literature and the opportunity to "go through all the provinces and converse freely with the Chinese of all ranks." Kant pointed out the difficulty of drawing conclusions from mutually contradictory ethnographic accounts, some of which argue for the intellectual superiority of Europeans and others whose evidence for the equal natural abilities of Africans and Native Americans was just as plausible. Aware of the limits of their knowledge, the best of Enlightenment thinkers urged caution and skepticism in reading empirical descriptions of non-European peoples. Yet they were fiery in criticizing the self-serving prejudices that fed politically motivated accounts. Here is Diderot on the Spanish conquest of Mexico:

> They fancied that these people had no form of government because it was not vested in a single person; no civilization because it differed from that of Madrid; no virtues because they were not of the same religious persuasion; and no understanding because they did not adopt the same opinions.[24]

Those words, like many others, were published anonymously, a reasonable precaution in order to avoid repeating the imprisonment Diderot had already suffered for earlier writings. Not every Enlightenment author was so lucky. Today Christian Wolff's name is known only to scholars, but in the early eighteenth century he was the most famous philosopher in Germany, and a major influence on the young Immanuel Kant. Yet in 1723 he was given forty-eight hours' notice to vacate his professorship at Halle, and the territory of Prussia, or face execution. His crime? Wolff had publicly argued that the Chinese were perfectly moral even without Christianity. His experience was no exception: nearly all the canonical Enlightenment texts were banned, burned, or published anonymously. However different they were, all were seen to threaten established authority in the name of universal principles available to anyone in any culture. Seventy years later, when the elderly Immanuel Kant was known as Germany's greatest philosopher and dubbed the Sage of Konigsberg, he was ordered to stop writing or speaking publicly about any question of religion. The Prussian professor obeyed the order until the minister who had issued it was replaced.

But the Enlightenment was the ideology of colonialism!
Do those who make this claim imagine there was no colonialism before the Enlightenment? Presumably not, but it's important to understand how something so false could come to seem true. (Raise a glass to the virtue of trying to understand those you disagree with.) Let's start with the fact that empires were not invented by the modern European nations whose advanced ships and guns were more effective in maintaining them

Universalism and Tribalism

than forced marches and pikes. Stronger nations have colonized weaker ones since the beginning of recorded history; indeed, before there were nations in our sense at all. Greeks and Romans built empires, as did the Chinese, the Assyrians, the Aztecs, the Malians, the Khmer, and the Mughals. Those empires operated with varying degrees of brutality and repression, but all of them were based on an equation of might and right, which amounts to no concept of right at all. All of them used their power to compel weaker groups to surrender resources, submit tribute, press soldiers into service for further imperial wars, and accept commands that overrode local custom and law. As far as we know, there was one thing they lacked: a guilty conscience.

Emperors who were particularly cruel might be criticized, though brutal practices in colonized lands were rarely attacked by those in the home states. Objections to Nero or Caesar usually focused on their crimes against Romans. The sixteenth-century Dominican friar Bartolomeo de las Casas was an early exception. His *Short Account of the Destruction of the Indies* denounced the atrocities that the Spanish conquest visited on indigenous peoples. But Las Casas argued for a kinder, gentler form of colonization, which included substituting African for South American slave labor. He never questioned the imperial project as a whole.

The Enlightenment did. Here is Kant's stinging attack on colonialism:

> Compare the inhospitable actions of the civilized and especially of the commercial states of our part of the world. The injustice they show to lands and peoples they visit (which is equivalent to conquering them) is carried by them

to terrifying lengths. America, the lands inhabited by the Negro, the Spice Islands, the Cape, etc., were at the time of their discovery considered by these civilized intruders as lands without owners, for they counted the inhabitants as nothing ... [they] oppress the natives, excite widespread wars among the various states, spread famine, rebellion, perfidy, and the whole litany of evils which afflict mankind. China and Japan, who have had experience with such guests, have wisely refused them entry.[25]

Though he was hardly a graceful writer, Kant was usually careful with words. He rarely used the word 'evil,' yet here he is crystal clear: colonialism creates every kind of evil that affects humankind. And while he praises the wisdom of China and Japan in closing their doors to European invaders, his critique of colonialism is not confined to the conquest of ancient, sophisticated cultures. At a time when nascent colonial powers justified their seizure of indigenous territories in Africa and the Americas by claiming those lands were unoccupied, their peoples uncivilized, Kant decried the injustice that "counted the inhabitants as nothing."

Diderot went even further, arguing that indigenous peoples threatened by European colonizers would have reason, justice, and humanity on their side if they simply killed the invaders like the wild beasts those intruders resembled. The Hottentots, he urged, should not be fooled by the false promises of the Dutch East Indian Company which had recently founded Cape Town.

> Fly, Hottentots, fly! ...Take up your axes, bend your bows, and send a shower of poisoned darts against these strangers. May there not be one of them remaining to convey to his country the news of their disaster. [26]

Universalism and Tribalism

Update the weaponry and you would be forgiven for thinking you'd come upon a quote from Frantz Fanon. Nor is this passage unusual: the eighteenth-century philosopher called for anti-colonialist violence at least as often, and often more dramatically, than the twentieth-century psychiatrist.

Enlightenment critics of empire didn't simply point out its cruelty. They also deconstructed the theories that sought to justify the theft of indigenous lands and resources. The most important of those theories was John Locke's labor theory of value, which was used to argue that nomadic peoples had no claim to the lands on which they hunted and gathered. According to Locke, people only acquire property through agriculture, mixing their labor with the land they work and thereby obtaining ownership. Kant disagreed:

> If those people are shepherds or hunters (like the Hottentots, the Tungusi, or most of the American Indian nations) who depend for their sustenance on vast open stretches of land, (foreign) settlement may not take place by force but only by contract, and indeed by contract that does not take advantage of the ignorance of those inhabitants with respect to ceding their lands.[27]

Here Kant not only undercut Locke's theory of property, but called out the shameless exploitation of peoples who, having no concept of private property in land, might cede the island of Manhattan for a handful of beads. Later critics dismissed this argument against settler colonialism as proof that Kant was unable to judge cultural or historical matters, since "primitive peoples" lacked concepts of right and were thus incapable of entering into treaties.

Universalism and Tribalism

If the best of Enlightenment thinkers denounced the vast theft of lands that made up European empires, what did they make of the vast theft of peoples? Most were unequivocal in condemning slavery. Kant's categorical imperative, which expresses the basic moral law, states that people should never be treated as means. This rules out slavery and other forms of oppression. These thinkers also lambasted European complicity in maintaining it, even by those who were not themselves slaveholders. Voltaire's *Candide* portrays an African in Surinam whose leg was cut off after his attempt to escape from slavery. "That's the price of your eating sugar in Europe," says the enslaved man. Diderot, going further, thought the enslavers would not be moved by pity or moral reasoning, and concluded that enslaved Africans must liberate themselves by violence. His prediction that "a great man, a Black Spartacus" would eventually arise to lead this liberation inspired Toussaint L'Ouverture. Kant took aim at religious claims invented to justify racialized slavery; long before the American Confederacy, it was argued that black people were descended from Ham, that son of Noah cursed for uncovering his father's nakedness. Against such dubious theology Kant used reason:

> Some people imagine that Ham is the father of the Moors and that God made him as a punishment which now all his descendants have inherited. However, one can provide no proof as to why the color black should be the mark of a curse in a more fitting fashion than the color white.[28]

Curiously enough, this passage was included in a recent volume of writings collected to reveal Enlightenment racism. The editor seems not to have noticed that

Universalism and Tribalism

Kant demolished an argument that White Supremacist Christians support to this day.[29]

Like progressive intellectuals everywhere, radical Enlightenment thinkers were only partially successful. While they changed the thinking of their contemporaries on many questions, they did not stop the great European rush for empire that gathered full force in the nineteenth century. This strand of thought went out of favor as the new century continued, and even liberal thinkers like John Stuart Mill championed moderate versions of imperialism.

Yet if they did not stop colonialism, they succeeded in giving it a bad conscience. As Jean-Paul Sartre wrote:

> A few years ago, a bourgeois colonialist commentator found only this to say in defense of the West: "We aren't angels. But we, at least, feel some remorse." What a confession![30]

The Romans felt no remorse or need to justify their empire. Nor did they tell their subjects that being colonized was good for them. In addition to better ships and weapons, nineteenth-century colonizers had something earlier imperialists lacked: a need for legitimacy. The nineteenth-century Indian nationalist Aurobindo Ghose put the matter thus:

> The idea that despotism of any kind was an offence against humanity had crystallized into an instinctive feeling ... Imperialism had to justify itself to this modern sentiment and could only do so by pretending to be a trustee of liberty, commissioned from on high to civilize the uncivilized.[31]

This, sadly, must be the source of the legend that the Enlightenment sanctioned colonialism. Enlightenment

Universalism and Tribalism

thinkers blasted colonialism and argued that justice was on the side of those non-European nations who killed or closed their doors to would-be invaders. A half century later, when faced with a powerful critique in the name of ideals they wanted for themselves, European imperialists sought ways to uphold ideals of liberty and self-determination at home while continuing to violate them abroad. Their solution was to claim they were bringing those ideals to those unable to realize them on their own. Empire, they argued, was a burden undertaken for the sake of the natives. Far from being in tension with the goods they cherished for their own folk – an end to famine and sickness and inequality before the law – all the colonialists sought to do was to bring those goods, plus Christianity, to benighted peoples who hadn't yet discovered them. Rousseau and Diderot and Kant would have seen through the scam – and wept to watch their own ideals turned into ideology. But the plunder was tempting, and its critics were dead.

There are scattered offensive remarks about blacks and Jews in the texts of even the greatest Enlightenment authors. Enlightenment thinkers were men of their time; most who left us records *were* men, and sexist men at that. They were educated by men of earlier times, and their struggle to free themselves of prejudice and preconception could never be final. Kant never noticed the contradictions between his occasional racist comments and his systematic theory. But it's fatal to forget that thinkers like Rousseau, Diderot, and Kant were not only the first to condemn Eurocentrism and colonialism. They also laid the theoretical foundation for the universalism upon which all struggles against racism must stand, together with a robust assurance that cultural pluralism is not an alternative to universalism but an enhancement of it. I like to think their belief in the possibility of progress would have led them to cheer our steps forward to insights they didn't attain. They were champions of reason, and anything else would be inconsistent.

While it's easy to find strongly anti-racist and anti-imperialist positions in the writings of most important Enlightenment thinkers, hardly any of them questioned sexism. If they saw no essential differences between European and non-European men, most of them assumed that biological differences between men and women determined entirely different destinies. The assumption seems less gratuitous when we recall that they lived at a time when childbirth was often fatal, and high infant mortality meant the average woman had to bear five children for the species to survive. Still, their remarks about women are often offensive enough that some will ask why we should take such thinkers seriously. But *pace* Audre Lorde, sometimes you need the master's tools to dismantle the master's house. That reason which most Enlightenment thinkers denied to women is one tool we cannot live without. Yet rather than critically engaging with it, reason itself is now identified with oppression.

It's no surprise you'd defend the Enlightenment and the universality of its universalism. That's just what the Enlightenment does: invent white European concepts and claim they apply to everyone.

What once was called *ad hominem* is now called positionality. You may question epistemological standpoints that reduce thinking to by-products of lived experience.

Universalism and Tribalism

Still I'm happy to state mine. I spent most of my life in the U.S. and Europe, and I code as a white woman. Though white nationalists don't think Jews count as white people, black nationalists do. For most Jews: it's complicated. As such I doubtless have particular biases, if only as frames of reference. The fact that I've written quite a lot about Immanuel Kant could be read as an attempt to rationalize those biases, or to think through my positions. No argument will decide that question.

For the sake of argument, then, it's worth turning briefly to non-white and non-European thinkers who share my conviction that universalism is not a fraudulent European imposition. The following remarks are not a survey but an invitation to further reading, since the thinkers I will mention are less well-known than the ones they oppose. Ibram X. Kendi sells more books than Adolph Reed, Achille Mbembe is more famous than Ato Sekyi-Otu, Gayatri Spivak better known than Benjamin Zachariah. Sometimes intellectual trends reflect accidental circumstances, but I suspect these do not. A preference for tribalism over universalism is not, in these cases, just a preference for particularity over generality. More importantly, it reflects the assumption that the victim's voice is the most authentic. Initially, the assumption seems justified. People may inflate their heroic qualities, exaggerate their achievements, cover up their cowardice. Heroes, above all, are contested. But as Wittgenstein said, "Try doubting in a real case if someone is in pain."[32] The great Austrian philosopher died, however, as the movement that shifted the historical subject from hero to victim was just beginning. Could he have imagined the claims of Donald Trump or Vladimir Putin to be history's victims?

Universalism and Tribalism

The valorization of the victim is widespread in contemporary Germany, the first nation in the world to begin a thoroughgoing reckoning with its historical crimes. That reckoning was slow, fitful, and often unwilling, but by the twenty-first century it produced a national consensus: guilt for the Holocaust is central to any narrative of German history. There's no doubt that this progressive move was an improvement on all the possible alternatives. Yet, by making the relationship between Jewish victims and German perpetrators central to Germany's self-image, Germans became unable to view Jews as anything but victims.

There are exceptions. But the unstated view that the voice of pain is the most authentic leads Germans to prioritize those Jewish nationalist voices focused on Jewish victimhood. The impulse is generous, if somewhat masochistic; guilt, in this case, is not exactly out of place. But that guilt has led Germans to ignore the voices of Jewish universalists – those of us who cannot shake the intuition that Palestinians, being human, have human rights that should be recognized. It was the universalist tradition in Judaism that produced the giants of German-Jewish culture, from Moses Mendelssohn to Hannah Arendt. And, though Mendelssohn's tombstone was desecrated, and Arendt was forced to flee the country, today's Germany honors such figures with everything from museum exhibits to postage stamps. (It's hard to find a contemporary German politician who has *not* quoted Arendt.) Yet educated Germans are often puzzled and surprised to learn that there is a Jewish universalist tradition at all, though its roots are in the Bible itself.

A similar process is at work in the changing relationships between white people and people of color. Woke movements deserve praise for making many people aware that even for genuine universalists, universal was more often colored white than brown, gendered male rather than female, presumed straight rather than gay. It also brought the evils of colonialism to the forefront of Western historical consciousness. Though woke has yet to create the kind of international consensus around racism that now exists in Germany around the Holocaust, a growing sense of shame among educated white people is hard to ignore. Those who long overlooked the presence of systemic racism or the breadth of colonialism will have good reason to listen hardest to those who emphasize them most loudly.

If listening hard is always a good idea, listening to one kind of voice at the expense of others is always a mistake. In these cases, residual if subterranean racism plays a role. For most Germans, Jews remain the Other, as people of color remain the Other for most white people. When you experience every individual as an instance of the Other, it's hard to experience them as individuals, easy to view them as representations of a tribe. This makes it hard to imagine they might hold a position that isn't tribalist.

Where Europeans once posed as civilizers for non-European savages, some now reverse the binary, viewing non-European, especially indigenous peoples as the source of all the virtues, while Europeans have none. Don't take my word for it; here's the anticolonial theorist and fighter Amilcar Cabral, assassinated in 1973:

> Without any doubt, underestimation of the cultural values of African peoples, based upon racist feelings and upon the intention of perpetuating foreign exploitation of Africans,

Universalism and Tribalism

has done much harm . . . but blind acceptance of the values of the culture, without considering what presently or potentially regressive elements it contains, would be no less harmful to Africa than racist underestimation of African culture had been.[33]

White publishers, foundations and universities now often elevate tribalist voices from the Global South as German cultural authorities now elevate tribalist Jewish ones, from a lingering sense of remorse. In both cases, the remorse is understandable, even admirable. But if it leads to viewing tribalist thinkers as the only authentic ones, it should not be decisive.

Thinkers like Sekyi-Otu are resolutely anti-tribalist, arguing that

> . . . 'race' obstructs our perceptual horizon, distracts us from attending to other, foundational questions of human *being* and social existence, so we should move on to those other questions, questions we would still have to address were the domination of racist culture as a world system ever to come to its long overdue end.[34]

There are tribalist writers, like the Afropessimist Frank Wilderson, who insist that the question of race *is* the foundational question of human being. They are unlikely to be persuaded by Sekyi-Otu. This does not make voices like Wilderson's more authentic. Cries of pain deserve a hearing and a response, but they are no more privileged a source of authority than careful arguments.

The philosopher Olúfémi Táíwò, who defends the relevance of the Enlightenment project for contemporary Africa, presents strong arguments against the current inclination to decolonize everything. Far from viewing colonization as being the result of modern Western values, he argues that colonization was problematic precisely because those values were ignored. Where colonized peoples were concerned, Europeans discarded their own ideas of liberty, self-determination, government by the consent of the governed and even humanity itself. Centering the history of Africa on the history of its colonization makes that history a narrative of Africa's invaders. This leads to a denial of African agency, which was present even in the variety of complex responses to colonization itself. Táíwò points out that the Moorish colonization of Spain and Portugal is viewed as merely an episode in Iberian history, though it lasted much longer than European colonization of Africa. He urges Africans to consider colonization as one chapter of their history rather than the center of it, ". . . unless we grant that white supremacists are right and we are permanent children whose will is forever at the mercy of our erstwhile colonizers."[35]

While contemporary universalist thinkers of color are ignored, universalist elements of classic anti-racist and anti-colonialist thought are downplayed. Frantz Fanon, who heads the postcolonial canon, wrote mercilessly about European barbarism. Yet statements like these are rarely quoted:

> All forms of exploitation are identical because all of them are applied against the same object: the human being. [36]

Sekyi-Otu argues that Fanon championed universalism for the same reason he supported the purportedly Western idea of individualism. How could he do otherwise when he was sworn to dismantle racist systems that

Universalism and Tribalism

simultaneously deny human universality and personal individuality?[37]

Amilcar Cabral, who led the fight for Cape Verdean and Guinean independence, is known for encouraging his compatriots to undertake "a re-Africanization of our minds." At the same time he rejected the apotheosis of indigenous culture by pointing out banalities that many cultural theorists overlook:

> All culture is composed of essential and secondary elements, of strengths and weaknesses, of virtues and failings, of factors of progress and factors of stagnation or regression.[38]

Instead of dismissing every cultural concept suspected as European, Cabral argued for adopting from other cultures "everything that has a universal character, in order to continue growing with the endless possibilities of humanity."[39] It's a thought that resonates with the final sentence of Fanon's *Wretched of the Earth*:

> For Europe, for ourselves, and for humanity, comrades, we must turn over a new leaf, we must work out new concepts and try to set afoot a new humanity.

What are needed, Fanon argued, are new concepts of humanity, and the related concept of universalism, to remove the taint of imperialist, fraudulent versions of those ideas. But, to reject universalism altogether because it has been abused, is to give Europe "the last word of the imperial act."[40]

It's the truth of universalism that makes what's now called cultural appropriation possible. Take two qualities that I called fundamentally human: the ability to feel pain, the desire for freedom. We recognize these feelings instinctively in others as well as in ourselves. Indeed, as

Universalism and Tribalism

observers have long noted, many mammals recognize them in other species. We may learn to extinguish the recognition for others, but it can be reignited. Nothing expresses pain, or the longing for freedom, more immediately than art in all its forms; this is one reason why the current suggestion that cultures belong to tribes is so misguided. Proscriptions on cultural appropriation assume a kind of cultural purity few objects ever have. Even in ancient times, art was traded and influences were blended until it was often impossible to tell which tribe was the object's owner – if ownership is the right model for culture at all. In *The Lies That Bind,* Appiah argues that it isn't. We can go a step further: viewing cultural productions as tribal commodities is a way to negate culture's liberating power.

In the antebellum South, slaveholders went so far as to rewrite the Bible so the story of Moses and the Exodus would not appear. They knew it was incendiary. As did enslaved African Americans, whose magnificent song "Go Down, Moses" made up for their restricted access to texts. Was that cultural appropriation, or what literary scholar Michael Rothberg calls multidirectional memory? Paul Robeson's worldview was grounded in his experience as the son of a man who escaped from American slavery. What moved him to political activism, however, was an encounter with striking Welsh miners singing on a London street. Nothing connects members of different tribes better than being moved by a cultural product; nothing offers more insight or stirs more emotion. Most of us know, though we're able to forget it, that members of other tribes feel pain and seek freedom just as we do. The arts can turn a piece of banal knowledge into a truth that

Universalism and Tribalism

has the power to move us, when a hundred propositions leave us cold.

Of course cultural appropriation should not be confused with cultural exploitation. Attempts to underpay artists for the work they create should be resisted like any other form of profiteering. But woke insistence on a tribal understanding of culture is not far enough from a Nazi insistence that German music should only be played by Aryans, or Samuel Huntington's insistence on defending what he calls Western culture against the threat of destruction by other civilizations.[41] To censure cultural appropriation is to sabotage cultural force.

When I bought Maya Angelou's *Life Doesn't Frighten Me*, with illustrations by Basquiat, as a third birthday present for one of my daughters, I wasn't conscious of giving her a lesson. Decades later, during the BLM demonstrations that prompted discussions and activism in so many families, she told me I had – precisely because I didn't accompany the gift with a lecture on antiracism or the value of diversity. The lesson I didn't give her went something like this: *members of other tribes are not the alien Other, but individuals who have thoughts and feelings like you.* Angelou's message to face danger without fear resounded to become my daughter's favorite story. Some things are better to show than to tell.

Great adult literature always renders the universal in the particular. How else could so many of us come to care about Tolstoy's chronicles of the intricacies of Russian aristocracy, Achibie's portrait of a village boy in war-torn Nigeria, Roy's tale of love doomed by caste in Kerala? Even good television can have that effect: who knew that millions of people could be transfixed by the struggles of a fictitious Danish politician?

Universalism and Tribalism

A distinction between culture and politics may help explicate my metaphor of flesh and bones. Cultural differences can be cherished, both by members of the culture doing the creating and those who appreciate them. Those differences are what make us interesting. It's not accidental that Esperanto was a failure. Though the intentions of those who strove to create a universal language were admirable, Esperanto lacked the rhythms and resonances that bind us to our native tongues. Even linguistically gifted learners rarely rise to the level of ease with a language that makes a native speaker feel at home.

Those who make the effort to enter another language or culture do, however, gain something invaluable: illumination of the world from another perspective: insight that their own perspective is inevitably partial; and visceral awareness of our common humanity. But if culture is particular, politics needs a universal core. Cultural differences can be treasured without being reified. A world without cultural difference would be as grim as an assembly of skeletons. But when we think and act politically, cultural categories should not take center stage.

At their best, cultural and political categories can reinforce each other. Cultural pluralism strengthens political solidarity, for the more you know of another culture, the more your sympathy for it is bound to grow. Even walking awhile in the steps of a culture that isn't yours will reveal your common humanity, and strengthen your commitment to universalism. For the best forms of art lead us to what Aime Cesaire called "a universal enriched by every particular,"[42] a universalism learned with and through difference.

3
Justice and Power

Imagine a bunch of guys passing time in a rich man's house. Time is what they have on their hands: they're waiting for nightfall, when a festival performance will begin nearby. It's the latest foreign thing, cutting-edge, sound and light. Easy to persuade those who have seen everything in town to try some new entertainment. Their initial conversation is innocuous; talk of death, sex, and money creates no friction. Only when they reach the subject of morality do sparks start to fly.

The conflict begins when the host names the real benefit of wealth: not the comfort and pleasure his guests are enjoying, but the fact that inherited money reduces the temptation to corruption. A rich man has no reason to deceive or defraud. He always pays his debts, and knows he can rest in peace.

This leaves an opening for one guest's favorite sport. He's smarter than the others, though he likes to humble-brag. He is happiest when demolishing other people's arguments. *Speaking of wealth and corruption: what's justice, after all? Just speaking the truth and paying your*

Justice and Power

debts? Is that what we owe everyone? What about a friend who has lost his mind?

Others step up to offer better definitions of justice, or virtue – it's never quite clear which is at issue. Justice, says one, is helping your friends and hurting your enemies. This is how the world often works, and not only in American foreign policy, but our know-it-all shows how the definition breaks down. He might conclude that seeking definitions of moral concepts is a mistake, but before he can count the implications the youngest listener blows up. When the others pause for breath he rushes at the speaker, wild like a beast.

Bullshit, he roars. How dim can they be? Why waste time debating the nature of justice when the whole idea is a sham? Don't they know that justice is nothing but a mask for the interest of the stronger?

The know-it-all does what he can to demolish that claim. But he's much better at attacking others' positions than defending his own, and his arguments are hard to follow. Increasingly impatient with pedantry, the young man resorts to verbal force: he calls the older man a baby. For only a baby believes that a shepherd feeds his sheep for their benefit. The rest of us know the shepherd's care reflects his own interest entirely: the fatter the sheep, the more the slaughterhouse will pay. The metaphor is no accident: rulers, he continues, regard their subjects like sheep. Consider tyranny over nations, or even private contracts: the just man always loses to the interests of the stronger. Most everyone knows this, and if everyone condemns injustice, it's not for fear of committing it but for fear of becoming its victims. For once in his life, our wise guy panics. Though he recovers enough to argue the younger man

Justice and Power

into blushing silence, he admits he cannot say what justice is.

It takes little effort to imagine such a conversation. Most readers of this book will have experienced one like it. The arguments should be familiar. *Talk of justice is just a smokescreen; what moves the real world is power.* The claim can be supported with a host of examples, for nothing is easier than naming a politician who preaches what she does not practice in order to lull her subjects into silence. Indeed, it's harder to find one who doesn't.

The claim that the rhetoric of justice has served to legitimate a grab for power *can* be part of a demand for justice. You might unmask that rhetoric in order to reverse the deed it concealed. If it's too late for that, you might urge that the perpetrators be called to account for their crimes, as well as their abuse of moral language, which sows doubt about its authority. The Iraq war would have been a good place to start. Among the other things that war has to answer for: its bombastic use of terms like "moral clarity" to disguise a war undertaken in search of oil, regional hegemony, and distraction from what was, at the time, considered the worst presidency in American history. Coming at the start of the twenty-first century, its glaring abuse of words like 'democracy' and 'freedom' magnified doubt that such words can ever be uttered in good faith. What's notable about the kind of discussion I've outlined is that it's *not* a demand for justice, but rather a claim that such demands are passé. Nor is it accidental that it doesn't take place in a slum or a slave yard, where questions about power and justice are ripe for the asking. It occurs in a home of wealth and abundance; you can almost smell the wine. Significantly, the indignant young man doesn't call for a change of power relations. All he requests concerns his own interest: he'd like to be paid for his performance. He is, at least, consistent.

Richard Rorty concluded,

> ... (this) is exactly the sort of left that the oligarchy dreams of, a left whose members are so busy unmasking the present that they have no time to discuss what laws need to be passed to create a better future.[1]

Rorty was criticizing what he called the Foucauldian academic left. I was paraphrasing the opening of Plato's *Republic*, the first great systematic work of Western philosophy. It is written in the voice of Socrates, who spends the rest of the dialogue trying to answer Thrasymachus, that postmodern young man who has survived several millennia. Each reincarnation is convinced that he is offering a bold and original revelation: human affairs in general, and politics in particular, are nothing but self-serving strategies to conceal raw power struggles. Each reincarnation exudes the same mixture of disappointment, indignation, and self-assurance: having discovered that the world doesn't live up to the claims that are made for it, he's determined to fall for no claims at all. Like his contemporary heirs, Thrasymachus sounds hard-headed, but the position is very easy; maintaining it requires no more than expounding an occasional critique. Isn't it clear that any attempt to work for more justice is worse than futile, downright absurd?

As the *Republic* shows, this sort of deflationary argument is anything but new; philosopher Bernard Williams called it ancient.

Justice and Power

It consists in taking some respected distinctions between the 'higher' and the 'lower' such as those between reason and persuasion, argument and force, truthfulness and manipulation, and denying the higher element while affirming the lower: everything, including argument or truthfulness, is force, persuasion and manipulation (really). This trope has its uses ... But besides the fact that it soon becomes immensely boring, it has the disadvantage that it does not help one to understand those idealizations.[2]

Still less, Williams continues, does it explain the differences between listening to someone and being hit by him.

Although both proclaim the primacy of power, Foucault's account of power's mechanisms is very different from that of Thrasymachus. The Greek sophist lived at a time when the powerful and the powerless were two clear and distinct subjects, a time that lasted, according to Foucault, through the eighteenth century. In principle, if seldom in practice, something like liberation was still possible: cut off the sovereign's head and his subjects might, for a moment, escape subjugation. In the modern era, said Foucault, power is hidden and diffuse, expressed through a network of structures we rarely perceive. There is no point we can locate and challenge, especially since we are implicated in the very networks that constrain us.

Even Foucault's sharpest critics acknowledge that this portrait describes something important about contemporary society. Our sense that we are dominated by a web of institutions that were neither designed nor controlled by anyone in particular is surely the source of the willingness to accept Foucault's wilder claims. As Michael Walzer wrote:

Justice and Power

> For it is Foucault's claim, and I think he is partly right, that the discipline of a prison, say, represents a continuation and intensification of what goes on in more ordinary places – and wouldn't be possible if it didn't. So we all live to a time schedule, get up to an alarm, work to a rigid routine, live in the eye of authority, are periodically subject to examination and inspection. No one is entirely free from these new forms of social control. It has to be added, however, that subjection to these new forms is not the *same thing* as being in prison: Foucault tends systematically to underestimate the difference.[3]

Foucault's discussions of how some forms of power work can be riveting. His readers inevitably hope that those analyses will be not merely interesting but, like any other critique of power, also liberating. But such hopes will be dashed by Foucault's view of what analyses, and knowledge more generally, can do:

> All knowledge rests on injustice (that there is no right, not even in the act of knowing, to truth or a foundation for truth) and that the instinct for knowledge is malicious (something murderous, opposed to the happiness of mankind).[4]

Small wonder many have concluded that the man was simply a nihilist.[5] Yet "no single analytic framework has saturated the field of colonial studies as completely as that of Foucault."[6] This is true, though he never addressed decolonialization, despite the omnipresence of the French war in Algeria as he was coming to professional maturity. Still, Edward Said was but one of many who saw him as "an apostle of radicalism and intellectual insurgency."[7] Everything in his performance screamed *rebel*. He wrote books that glorified those on society's margins: the outlaw, the madman. He often took political stands that supported the oppressed, be they convicts in French prisons or victims of the military dictatorship in Chile. And decades before anyone began to imagine marriage equality, he was openly, transgressively gay. Why shouldn't Foucault become the bedrock of left-wing thought, or at least the one philosopher read by anyone who isn't a philosopher, as Sartre was for an earlier generation? Those now teaching students were students themselves during his heyday in the 1980s and 1990s, and they pass on the texts they learned as exciting new classics.

Those texts contain fascinating descriptions of the development of prisons, psychiatric clinics, schools, and other institutions crucial to expanding social power. Many historians are grateful to Foucault for opening avenues of exploration that were once consigned to the margins, if they were studied at all. But, while reading Foucault on the particular, students are absorbing a philosophical lesson that's very general: power, only vaguely tied to the actions of particular humans in particular institutions, is the driving force of everything. "Power is everywhere," he wrote. "Power produces reality, it produces domains of objects and rituals of truth." For the late Foucault, power was embedded in every feature of modern life. Power was woven into the very fabric of our language, thoughts, and desires. Power even enfolds resistance, which reinforces power. It's power all the way down.

If power is so ubiquitous, you may wonder if it serves to demarcate at all. If everything is power, does the concept have no bounds? Anyone who hoped

Justice and Power

that Foucault's idea of power might prove to be so broad as to become innocuous will be dismayed by his explication:

> I believe one's point of reference should not be to the great model of language and signs, but to that of war and battle. The history which bears and determines us has the form of a war rather than that of a language: relations of power, not relations of meaning . . . 'Dialectic' is a way of evading the always open and hazardous reality of conflict by reducing it to a Hegelian skeleton, and 'semiology' is a way of avoiding its *violent, bloody* and *lethal* character by reducing it to the calm Platonic form of language and dialogue. [italics added][8]

There is nothing soft in Foucault's concept of power:

> Isn't power simply a form of warlike domination? Shouldn't one therefore conceive all problems of power in terms of relations of war? Isn't power a sort of generalized war which assumes at particular moments the forms of peace and the state? Peace would then be a form of war, and the state a means of waging it.[9]

An introductory course in logic could have prevented some confusion. From the fact that some moral claims are hidden claims to power, you cannot conclude that every claim to act for the common good is a lie. But logic is seldom the strong point of Thrasymachus' heirs. As Foucault does in this passage, they tend to avoid declarative sentences; the metaphysics of suspicion is better served by asking questions. And though they are usually fond of Nietzsche, their writing is sufficiently obscure to merit one of his better put-downs: "They muddy the waters to make them seem deep."

Is there anything, on Foucault's account, that isn't power? One concept is clearly ruled out; power is not justice. More exactly, Foucault insisted that the idea of justice itself was invented as a weapon against certain forms of political and economic power. "If justice is at stake in a struggle, then it is as an instrument of power; it is not in the hope that finally one day, in this or another society, people will be rewarded according to their merits, or punished according to their faults."[10] To deny the latter is just to deny the essence of justice, whether human or divine, in any culture: justice always seeks to reward people according to merit, punish them according to fault. Every time we protest an injustice, we protest an imbalance between virtue and happiness. Asked about his engagement in prison reform, Foucault replied that he was not interested in the banalities of prison conditions but wanted to "question the social and moral distinction between the innocent and the guilty." This is not a distinction that prisoners themselves would question; rather, they insist on it.[11] Anyone who denies the moral distinction between innocence and guilt denies the possibility of moral distinctions at all.

The above quotes are taken from a debate between Foucault and Noam Chomsky that was aired on Dutch television in 1971. The Vietnam war was still raging, and Marxist ideas of revolution were matters for serious discussion on European television. Chomsky avowed he would only support a revolutionary proletariat that promoted a just society; were a revolution to turn terrorist, he wanted out. Here is Foucault's reply: "The proletariat makes war with the ruling class because, for the first time in history, it wants to take power. One makes war to win, not because it is just." Nor did he flinch from implications: When the proletariat takes power, it may exert violent, dictatorial, and bloody power toward the classes over which it has triumphed. "I can't see what objection one could make to this," he continued. Chomsky later remarked that Foucault was the most amoral man he ever met.

Foucault disguised the force of his general views beneath a false modesty that claimed the age of "general intellectuals" like Sartre had passed, and that what was required now were the findings of "specific intellectuals," like himself. He steadfastly refused to give reasons for his political judgments, claiming that reasons were nothing but self-serving rationalizations.

The insistence that power is the only driving force goes hand in hand with contempt for reason. It's impossible to say which came first, the demotion of reason or the promotion of power; they form two sides of an argument. Twentieth-century thinkers as different as Foucault, Heidegger, and Adorno were united in viewing what they called "Enlightenment reason" not merely as a self-serving fraud but even more as a domineering, calculating, rapacious sort of monster committed to subjugating nature – and with it, indigenous peoples considered to be natural. On this picture, reason is merely instrument and expression of power. Williams' distinction between being persuaded by someone and being beaten by them becomes spurious; reason is a more polite but more manipulative way of hitting someone over the head. (Améry would say that those who find the distinction meaningless have never been beaten.) Those assumptions about the Enlightenment's conception of reason are no more accurate than the assumption that the Enlightenment was Eurocentric. My book *Moral Clarity* discusses Enlightenment notions of reason at length; here I will only respond to the most common charges.[12]

The idea that reason is hostile to nature rests on a binary opposition between reason and nature no Enlightenment thinker would have accepted. The two can seem to conflict because reason's ability to ask what is natural and what is not is the first step toward any form of progress. One major aim of Enlightenment study of non-European cultures was to question a host of European institutions. Their authority rested on church and state insistence that they were natural, hence immutable. Recall what was considered natural in the eighteenth century: slavery, poverty, the subjection of women, feudal hierarchies, and most forms of illness. Well into the nineteenth century, English clerics argued that attempts to relieve the Irish famine would defy God's order. Enlightenment thinkers were hardly opposed to nature or to passion – two topics they explored as fully as any other. But they knew how often oppression is justified by claims of supposed natural order, and they were determined to use reason to subject those claims to rigorous scrutiny. Every time you argue that an economic, racial or gender inequality is not inevitable, you are using your reason to question those who insist inequalities are natural.

While reason is not averse to nature, it is opposed to received authority that defends its power by restricting thinking to a small elite. Defining reason as a matter of courage rather than knowledge was one way to insist on human equality: every peasant can think for herself, as every professor can fail. Reason and freedom are connected in more ways than one: knowledge was meant to liberate people from superstition and prejudice, instrumental reasoning from poverty and fear. Enlightenment philosophers were perfectly aware that reason has limits; they just weren't prepared to let church and state be the ones to draw them. We have inherited their ideas so thoroughly that we no longer recognize how radical they are, nor how sorely they are still needed. In an era of drastic censorship and widespread illiteracy, the claim that anyone of any station had a right to think was explosive, and church authorities used their considerable power to suppress it with force. Authorities today look different: economic experts proclaim *there is no alternative* to neoliberalism and support the alleged naturalness of their ideology with evolutionary theory. Enlightenment thinkers never thought reason was unlimited; they just refused to let authorities set the limits on what we can think.

Reason and logic are needed for the instrumental rationality required for finding the best means to an end, including technological solutions designed to prevent and cure illnesses, improve agriculture, save women and others from lifetimes of senseless toil. (That technology, like the sorcerer's apprentice, can run amok is not a problem we can solve by abolishing it.) But instrumental rationality is just the beginning of reason's scope. Reason's most important function is to uphold the force of ideals. Unless you can show that reality can be changed on the basis of ideas of reason, every demand for change will be dismissed as utopian fantasy. Such demands are often dismissed with condescension: your ideals are commendable, but the hard facts of experience speak against them. The claim was already a cliché in 1793, as Kant showed in his essay

"On the Old Cliche: That May be Right in Theory but it Won't Work in Practice." There he turns the claims of those who call themselves realists on their head. *Of course the ideas of reasons conflict with the claims of experience. That's what ideas do.* Ideals are not measured by how well they fit reality; reality is judged by how well it lives up to ideals. Reason's job is to deny that claims of experience are final – and to move us to widen the horizon of experience by providing ideals that experience ought to obey. If enough of us do so, it will.

Understood properly, reason is a demand: *for everything that happens find the reasons why it is so and not otherwise.* Reason enables us to go beyond whatever experience we are given, and allows us to think: *This could have been different, why is it like this?* The actual is given to us, but it takes reason to conceive the possible. Without that capacity we couldn't begin to ask why something is wrong, or imagine that it might be better. Philosophers call this the principle of sufficient reason. It is so fundamental that we can hardly imagine functioning without it, and we're likely to take it for granted, but the demand to find reasons is the basis of scientific research and social justice. Many things count as reasons, but some things do not: *My father told me. I heard it somewhere. That's just the way the world is.* The child follows the principle of sufficient reason when she asks *Why is it raining?* and continues inquiring until the adult supplies a satisfying answer – or tells her to stop asking questions. But unless she herself is destitute and assumes the condition is natural, the child will also wonder the first time she sees a homeless person. *Why is he sleeping on the sidewalk? Why doesn't he have a*

Justice and Power

home? Adults who are serious about giving an answer must move from explanation to action.

Reason does have the power to change reality, but to view it as *merely* a form of power is to ignore the difference between violence and persuasion, and between persuasion and manipulation. It's the difference between saying *you should do this because I'm bigger than you* and *you should do this because it's (a) right (b) good for the community (c) in your best interest (d) choose your own form of justification.* This is one of the first distinctions we teach our children. As we grow older we learn that most actions are undertaken for more than one reason, but overdetermination doesn't undermine the distinction between reason and brute force. Those who ignore it should undergo what Améry called a banality cure, therapy to overcome the fear of acknowledging the banal truths that frame our lives. For the distinction between reason and violence undergirds the distinction between democracy and fascism, and any hope of resisting the slide toward fascism depends on remembering the difference.

Even stranger than the progressives' embrace of Michel Foucault is their fascination with Carl Schmitt, though little in their styles was similar. As political scientist Alan Wolfe argued, "Schmitt's ideas loom so large over the contemporary left that one need not even refer to him in order to be influenced by him."[13] Where Foucault was flamboyant, courting outrage, Schmitt performed the persona of a conservative lawyer. His main transgression against the world in which he found himself was to reject any form of regret for the Nazi regime he'd loyally served. In writing, Foucault meandered, while Schmitt preferred short oracular pro-

Justice and Power

nouncements. Yet they shared rejections of the idea of universal humanity and the distinction between power and justice, along with a deep skepticism toward any idea of progress. What makes them both interesting to progressive thinkers today is their shared hostility toward liberalism and their commitment to unmasking liberal hypocrisies. It's not clear whether Foucault's unmasking had a purpose other than subversion as an art form. What's certain is that Schmitt's demasking of liberal institutions was undertaken for the greater glory of the Third Reich, both before and after the war.

Schmitt was a reactionary Catholic who rejected the reforms of Vatican II not only because he was attached to the Latin mass but because Pope John XXIII withdrew the historical claim that the church was "in perpetual enmity with Muslims and Jews."[14] For the creator of the hazy concept *political theology*, the Catholic Church was the archetypical political institution. He thought the defining distinction of politics is the contrast between friend and enemy, as morality is defined by the concepts of good and evil, aesthetics by the concepts of beautiful and ugly. In *Minima Moralia*, Adorno argued that Schmitt's friend/enemy schema objectifies the Other, fitting Nazi ideology perfectly. Perhaps even more telling: defining the political this way is regressive; Schmitt reduces the political to categories only a child would use.[15]

In Schmitt's later writings he sometimes made disclaimers: the friend/enemy distinction was not individual; it was a formal category, which could be applied without hatred. (He condemned the Cold War for introducing "the treatment of the Other as criminal, murderer, saboteur and gangster" – a claim that would be less incredible were it not written in Germany four years after WWII.)[16] But his attempt to soften his concept of enemy founders like Foucault's attempts to suggest a gentler notion of power. Both wrote too many passages welcoming the violent associations. Schmitt's readers today usually focus on earlier writings like *Political Theology* and *The Concept of the Political*, which are nebulous and portentous enough to imply many things. Surely he can't mean 'enemy' like the Nazis meant 'enemy'? But even in *The Concept of the Political*, Schmitt wrote that both

> ... war and politics are a matter of the most extreme and intense antagonisms ... The concepts of friend, enemy and struggle receive their real meaning especially insofar as they relate to and preserve the real possibility of political annihilation.[17]

And, though he argued that his concept of political enmity need not lead to killing, he also called Cain's murder of Abel the "beginning of the history of mankind."[18]

"When I battle in resistance against the Jews, I am fighting for the work of the Lord." Schmitt praised this quote of Hitler's in his 1936 essay "Die deutsche Rechtswissenschaft im Kampf gegen den jüdischen Geist." After all, the Jews fit the definition of political enemy he had formulated ten years earlier:

> He is the other, the alien, and it suffices that in his essence he is something existentially other and alien in an especially intensive sense.[19]

Had he confined his depiction of Jews as enemies to texts he wrote during the Third Reich, one might argue

– albeit not very plausibly – that he was under political pressure. That would make him a world-historical coward, but it could ground a claim that his famous friend/enemy distinction was something more abstract, and less vulgar, than anything the Nazis had in mind. Unfortunately for the Schmittians who make this argument, his pre- *and* post-war diaries display noxious antisemitism in vulgar and high-flown terms. Both biological and religious antisemitism played a role here, but antimodernism was even more important. Like Heidegger's notorious *Black Notebooks,* Schmitt's diaries treat Jews as emblems of everything he hated about the modern world.[20] So it's no surprise that his postwar diaries were full of comments like "Jews always remain Jews . . . precisely the assimilated Jew is the true enemy."[21]

In Germany there were Nazis, and there were Nazis. Some were committed to the ideology, most went along with the regime to advance their careers. Very few of either kind were genuinely contrite after 1945. They had lost the war, some seven million citizens and a third of their territory. Their cities were in ruins and occupied by foreign armies. Some of them, like Schmitt, were barred from practicing their professions, or even briefly jailed. The deaths of millions of civilians, they insisted, were just part of the tragedy of war. Human beings were born to sin. What about the firebombing of Dresden or the atomic Holocaust at Hiroshima?

Pernicious attitudes like these were very widespread, but rarely publicly defended. And though it took decades, many who held such views came to see they were, well, lacking in perspective. Carl Schmitt never did. He called denazification "terror" and demanded an amnesty in which Nazi crimes would not only be forgiven but forgotten. He wrote an essay called "The Tyranny of Values," which argued that values are entirely constructed, citing Heidegger, who dismissed values as "positivistic ersatz for the metaphysical."[22] Echoing Thrasymachus, he argues that values are inherently engines of political violence. Schmitt's goal in that essay, as historian Samuel Zeitlin has shown, was hardly a general defense of legal positivism, but a defense of the Nazi propagandist Veit Harlan. If values are empty positivistic categories, on what basis could Nazis be condemned? "The crimes against humanity are committed by the Germans. The crimes for humanity are committed against the Germans. That is the only difference."

It's been argued that Celine's literature can be dissociated from his support of fascism. It's been argued that Heidegger's Nazism should play no role in evaluating his metaphysics.[23] I don't agree with those arguments, but they are at least coherent. It's much harder to contend that we should take seriously the ideas of a *political theorist* who defended his commitment to Nazism forty years after the war was over, particularly when those ideas are congruent with, perhaps foundational to, Nazi ideology.

Harking back to the Christian doctrines of original sin which he never abandoned, Schmitt wrote that "all genuine political theories presuppose humankind to be evil." Thus conflict, he held, is the law of life. It's a view that Schmitt and his followers like to call realism, while disdaining every other as naive. It's rarely acknowledged that this implies a strong set of metaphysical claims about the nature of reality. Real things, on a Schmittian view, can be quantified and perceived with some combination of our senses. This leaves no room for ideas like justice, fairness or equality, but plenty of room for lands and seas, oil and grain, rockets and tanks. There's no way around it: this is a political theory for war. He contrasted the political sphere with the economic one, which he dismissed as a stale arena of negotiation and compromise – the sort of thing Anglo-Saxons do. What gives life real meaning, by contrast, is the distinction between friend and foe. Like Nietzsche on a bad day, Schmitt argued that the threat of violent death at the hands of the Other is the source of heroic virtues, and real men, who scorn the insipid pursuits that create vulgar trader mentalities.

What makes such a noxious worldview appealing? (He couldn't even write as well as Nietzsche.) Readers who situate themselves to the left of liberalism can only be attracted by Schmitt's stinging critiques of liberal failure and hypocrisy. He described liberal democratic parliaments as institutions that do nothing but endlessly talk, while real questions are decided elsewhere – a description that fits the twenty-first-century U.S. Congress as well as the Weimar Republic's *Reichstag*. It's even easier to agree with his critique of colonialism. The key to modern history, wrote Schmitt, is the European land-grab that took over the globe. He was particularly scorching about British imperialism: English pieties about humanity and civilization were nothing but rhetoric to disguise monumental acts of piracy. Americans fared no better. Schmitt attacked the Monroe Doctrine: framed as an opposition to European colonization of South America, it became a declaration that only the United States would determine what happens on the continent it considers its backyard. This justified critique didn't deter him, when writing on international law, from using the Monroe Doctrine as precedent to justify expanding the Greater German Reich. Note the year of publication: the book expounding these views was published in 1942, when Germany was at war with Britain and America. Every argument that undermined their claim to be fighting for justice or democracy was welcome.

Had we read *Mein Kampf* we would have seen this sort of thing before. Hitler himself used European Americans' genocide of Native peoples and theft of Native lands to justify his hope to extend German *Lebensraum* all the way to Vladivostok. Other Nazis played the same game when they responded to American protests against the Nurnberg Laws by posting pictures of American lynching of black people: take care of your own race problem before you lecture about ours. Neither Hitler, nor the Nazi lawyers who drew on racist American law were wrong: Britain and America were often committed to violent racist and colonial practices that were entirely at odds with their liberal democratic rhetoric. But Nazi use of these examples was hardly an effort at simple unmasking, let alone a contribution to liberation. Much like for Vladimir Putin today, their only interest was in the question: if the lofty lands of liberty engage in theft and terror, can't we do it too? Schmitt avoided answering the simple question *Do two wrongs make a right?* by arguing that in a world history saturated with violence, concepts like *right* and *wrong* disappear. Both are merely rhetoric used to disguise the only force there is: power. Significantly, while Schmitt's deconstruction of liberal democracies targeted Third Reich enemies, the Nazis rarely trumpeted his political theories. Even with universal conscription, it's hard to convince nineteen million men to risk their lives for what's merely an eternal struggle for power without some moral content. Schmitt was the Third Reich's leading legal theorist but not its leading propagandist. Appeals to defend their homeland from beastly Bolsheviks sustained far more Germans on the battlefield.

The concept of 'natural rights' is contested but, whatever else they may be, human rights are claims meant to curb naked assertions of power. They insist that power is not merely the privilege of the strongest person in the neighborhood; it demands justification. Remember the history in which claims to human rights arose: it was unthinkable that peasants and princes could stand anywhere on anything resembling equal footing. If the peasant took the prince's deer, he could be hanged. If the prince took the peasant's daughter, that was just the way the world was. The doctrine of the divine right of kings was less a doctrine than an assertion of God's power, and his ability to transfer that power to his representatives and their descendants. It's also worth recalling the theological background in which the doctrine of divine right arose. Millions of Europeans slaughtered each other in the wars of religion. Like most wars, those wars concerned territory and treasure, but they were also fought over theological questions. The most fraught conflicts concerned God's nature: was his power constrained by his goodness, or could God do whatever he pleased? Calvinists argued that God's power was absolute: if he consigned millions of babies to eternal hellfire, who were we to question him? Where that conception of God was on offer, it wasn't easy to constrain the power of earthly kings.

Universalist claims of justice meant to restrain simple assertions of power were often abused, from the American and French Revolutions that first proclaimed them to the present day. Carl Schmitt wasn't wrong about that. He concluded that unvarnished power grabs like those of the Nazis were not only legal but legitimate. You may think that's the best we can do. Or you may go to work to narrow the gap between ideals of justice and realities of power.

While Foucault may have added to our understanding of power in the modern world, I've argued that neither he nor Schmitt promoted a new view about the relations between justice and power. In simplest form their views go back to the Sophists: claims to justice are developed to disguise power-driven interests. It's a throwback to a world in which might – call it power – makes right, which amounts to no concept of right at all. What's new is the number of worldviews that take them for granted today. Because claims of justice have so often been used to conceal grabs for power, the line between power and justice is increasingly ignored. Thrasymachus' assumptions now appear inescapable, and anything else increasingly quaint. Given two equally plausible explanations of a piece of human behavior, we're inclined to converge on the worst. The more often you've been disappointed, the easier it is to expect disappointment. The more often you've been lied to, the easier it is to suspect manipulation behind everything you're told. The consequences of British imperialism and U.S. hegemony are still present enough to make Schmitt's critique ring true. Most now assume it's simply human nature to further your own interests *über alles,* and to disguise those interests with moral rhetoric.

If you ask for an argument, you are answered with history. And history hardly lacks examples of struggles for power dressed in fine clothes. Foucault and Schmitt show how many of the clothes are illusions. But a whole slew of naked emperors would only be *evidence* for dire claims about human nature and its possibilities; it wouldn't amount to proof. Even for those who believe in essences, proofs about the essence of human nature should have seemed impossible since 1756, when Jean-Jacques Rousseau taught us how thoroughly we read our own worldviews, and political hopes, into the prehistory we can never know.

Then along came evolutionary psychology. It didn't seem to be just another philosophy. It looked like hard science and purported to give us insight into the essence of our preliterate hunter-and-gatherer ancestors, who were too primitive to formulate rationalizations to describe their behavior, or at least to write them down. From these unprovable speculations about what (might have) led human beings to act (in that environment), evolutionary psychologists concluded that all human behavior is driven by our interest in maximizing our chances of reproduction: whatever we do is moved by the urge to perpetuate ourselves.

The historian of science Erika Milam shows that the theory was originally considered an advance on the leading evolutionary theories of the previous decade. Social scientists had failed to explain human violence during the Cold War, leading some researchers to turn to biology. They offered what was known as the killer ape theory. It claimed that humans are distinguished from other primates by a greater tendency to aggression, and that this aggression is the driving force behind human evolution. The view was popularized in several best-selling books as well as successful Hollywood movies, but soon came under attack for lack of evidence. Edward O. Wilson, the founding father of sociobiology, reversed the question on which the killer ape theory was based. If defenders of that theory had wondered how creatures evolved from a relatively peaceful past to the world-shaking violence of recent history, sociobiologists began by accepting their conclusions and assuming that humans had always been aggressively competitive. "I think Tennyson's 'nature red in tooth and claw' sums up our modern understanding of natural selection admirably," wrote evolutionary biologist Richard Dawkins. The real question, Wilson argued, was how we learned to cooperate at all when cooperation sacrificed our own genetic best interests. Sociobiologists were deeply puzzled by the undeniable fact that individuals sometimes sacrifice their own well-being to protect others. By asking how such altruism had evolved, Milam explains, sociobiologists naturalized violence as essential to human nature.

> Taking aggression for granted, sociobiologists sought to understand why animals ever cooperated, and in sexual selection and kin selection they thought they had answers. Sex, parenting and animal families might look like cooperation, but when males and females sexually unite, each unconsciously follows a competitive strategy evolved over many generations to give birth to the next generation and in doing so perpetuates his or her individual genetic lineage.[24]

The theory itself soon evolved to offer explanations not only of sex and family life but virtually everything we do. As anthropologist Clifford Geertz began one review:

> This is a book about "the primary male–female differences in sexuality among humans," in which the following things are not discussed: guilt, wonder, loss, self-regard, death, metaphor, justice, purity, intentionality, cowardice, hope, judgment, ideology, humor, obligation, despair, trust, malice, ritual, madness, forgiveness, sublimation, pity, ecstasy, obsession, discourse, and sentimentality. It could only be one thing, and it is. Sociobiology.[25]

Even its defenders occasionally admitted that "It seems ludicrous to suggest that all activities of humans derive from the reproductive strategies of individuals, or more properly their genes.[26] But those committed to finding a single framework to explain all human behavior pushed blithely on. It was not long before left-leaning critics attacked the political implications of sociobiology. Stephen Jay Gould, one of the earliest, wrote that

> Biological determinism has always been used to defend existing social arrangements as biologically inevitable ... from 19th century imperialism to modern sexism.[27]

Many elements of sociobiology were implicitly racist; since Wilson's death, even more explicit ties to racist biology have been uncovered. Feminist critics were indignant over the ways sociobiologists projected current gender roles into prehistory, thus implying that those roles are inevitable. Wilson responded to the critics by claiming he was not a biological determinist; hereditary traits merely delimit potential behavior, which may vary according to culture. But his examples of cultural variation were not very promising: men are genetically inclined to mate with as many women as possible but, depending on the culture, this may take the form of marriage plus mistresses, serial monogamy, or polygamy. Each cultural variation, however, presumes a monogamous woman at home tending the DNA. Those startled by this formulation should consider Wilson's "The organism is only DNA's way of making more DNA," a play on Samuel Butler's, "The chicken is only the egg's way of making another egg."

Some sociobiologists were careful to distinguish between "pop sociobiology" and serious studies in the field, but philosopher Philip Kitcher, who makes such distinctions, wrote that "The popular presentations are where the action is."[28] They are also, of course, the versions which seep into the general culture. Pop sociobiology, Kitcher continued,

> ... furthers the idea that class structures are socially inevitable, that aggressive impulses toward strangers are part of our evolutionary heritage, that there are ineradicable differences between the sexes that doom women's hopes for genuine equality."[29]

By the mid-1980s a consensus emerged: sociobiology was unsupported by evidence, and reactionary to boot. Sociobiologists protested that they were merely being realistic where their critics were sentimental. But the criticisms were so widespread that in their aftermath few wanted to use the name 'sociobiology' to describe anything involving the study of human behavior. Around the turn of the millennium, however, sociobiology re-emerged in a slightly less offensive form under a different name. Evolutionary psychologists acknowledged their debts to sociobiology but argued that their new field was better adapted to human beings through the addition of psychological categories. The revision added a layer of protection against the charge of biological reductionism, but it's largely a distinction without a difference. Kitcher calls evolutionary psychology "pop sociobiology with a fig leaf."[30] Most importantly, it does not change the fact that the mechanisms being selected are fundamentally selfish.

> Evolutionary biology is quite clear that 'What's in it for me?' is an ancient form for all life, and there is no reason to exclude *Homo sapiens*.[31]

As other philosophers have noted, evolutionary psychologists make a practice of slipping between different uses of the word "selfish." Sometimes they use it to imply exactly what we mean in ordinary conversation. Richard Dawkins begins his best-selling *The Selfish Gene* as follows:

> The argument of this book is that we, and all other animals, are machines created by our genes. Like successful Chicago gangsters, our genes have survived, in some cases for millions of years, in a highly competitive world ... I shall argue that a predominant quality to be expected in a successful gene is ruthless selfishness. However, there are special circumstances in which a gene can achieve its own selfish goals by fostering a limited form of altruism.

The reference to Chicago gangsters and the use of words like 'ruthless' invoke the sort of behavior you'd condemn in anyone you had the misfortune to meet. Under criticism, however, Dawkins and others reply they are not using the word 'selfish' in an ordinary vulgar sense, since genes can't be said to have motives at all. Rather, they are using the word to describe a complex abstract property, the tendency to maximize one's own gene representation in future generations. Yet the slide between the ordinary and the technical use of words like 'selfish' occurs again and again – along with elaborations that strongly suggest evolutionary psychologists intend 'selfish' to mean exactly what we think it means.

Thus no less than the sociobiologists who spawned them, evolutionary psychologists are faced with what they call the problem of altruism. For however many examples of dressed-up struggles for power and self-preservation history provides, it also gives us countless examples of people who sometimes do things that are counter to naked self-interest, even at the cost of their lives. The philosopher Mary Midgley argues that the claim of universal selfishness is incoherent: "Had regard for others really been impossible, there could have been no word for failing to have it."[32] Such examples pose a problem for the theory, but evolutionary psychologists work very hard to fit them into their schema. Wilson is clear about the principle:

> Altruism is ultimately selfish. The 'altruist' expects reciprocation from society for himself or his closest relatives. His good behavior is calculating, often in a wholly conscious way ... Its psychological vehicles are lying, pretense and deceit, including self-deceit, because the actor is most convincing who believes that his performance is real.[33]

Steven Pinker expands on Wilson's general claims:

> Community, the very different emotion that prompts people to sacrifice without an expectation of payback,

may be rooted in nepotistic altruism, the empathy and solidarity we feel toward our relatives, which evolved because any gene that pushed an organism to aid a relative would have helped copies of itself sitting inside that relative ... Sometimes it pays people (in an evolutionary sense) to love their companions because their interests are yoked, like spouses with common children ... sometimes it doesn't pay them at all, but their kinship-detectors have been tricked into treating their group-mates *as if* they were relatives by tactics like kinship metaphors (*fraternities, the Fatherland*).[34]

Suppose you ask why, in this account, we care about developing good character. The evolutionary psychologist will reply: *In the small villages we used to inhabit, your good deeds were noticed and remembered, so you could be sure of getting a piece of my pie someday if you gave me some of yours.* If you're convinced that sharing is driven by the desire for hedging your bets you will find this explanation convincing – at least until you ask why they cared about character in London or Beijing. *The behavior that was adaptive for small towns was carried over into large ones where it continued automatically even after it stopped producing immediate benefits.* Any problem in the theory can be explained by saying that what no longer serves our selfish interests once served our hunter-gatherer ancestors. This is faith-based speculation. It can be carried on without limit, down to all the times history showed human willingness to die for a principle. Why would good Darwinians do that? *Because even if they lose their own lives they may be maximizing the reproductive success of their kin.* And soldiers who die for their countries? *In earlier times, country used to be kin.* And people who die for something even more abstract? If you are already convinced that every bit of altruistic behavior is a disguised form of self-interest, you will find a way to argue that *it could have been self-interested* in the old days and went on spinning its idle wheels in ours. Surely you're not the sort of religious fundamentalist who refuses to believe Darwin?

Evolutionary psychologists often insinuate that any objections to their views are objections to science itself. They suggest that their critics, if not closet creationists, are nostalgic sentimentalists unable to accept Nietzsche's view that moral values like altruism died along with their creator. The rhetorical tone, writes Midgley,

> ... varies between reverence for (genetic) power and contempt for humans who suppose that any other element in life need concern them. It is strongly fatalistic, that is not just resigned to evils which have been proved inevitable but more generally contemptuous of all human effort.[35]

And as Kitcher concludes, the ideas being disguised have a long history:

> When we examine the pop sociobiological treatment of human altruism, it is found to dissolve into gratuitous Hobbesian speculations that have no basis in biology or any other science.[36]

Kitcher is hardly alone here. Among others, Friedrich Engels, Richard Lewontin and Donna Haraway note the Hobbesian war of all against all that sits at the bottom of most evolutionary theory. As Milam showed, the ubiquity of aggression for which the killer ape theory had argued became a starting point for sociobiology. While the speculations are found in Hobbes, they can be found even earlier, for the philosopher who wrote of natural life as "solitary, poor, nasty, brutish and short" was an early modern iteration of Thrasymachus. As Midgley writes:

> The underlying moral and psychological distortions really have not changed (since Spencer's misunderstandings of Darwin). The world-picture which this rhetoric displays is still the one crudely projected by those who glorified free-enterprise capitalism in its brash expansive stages by depicting both human nature and the biosphere as framed in its image. It is used now, as it was then, to justify the character faults typical of this cultural phase by treating them as universal and inevitable.[37]

She concludes, "In short, the deity being worshipped is power."

For the record: Darwin did show that the human species developed from ancestors we have in common with our evolutionary cousins, the great apes, but nothing in his work supports the claim that human action can be understood by examining apes' reproductive strategies. Though contemporary evolutionary psychologists usually avoid the more dramatically reductionist claims, their views work together to insinuate them. Not even the most passionate evolutionary theorist denies some difference between our reproductive strategies and those of a chimpanzee. The man who composes a sonnet for his beloved has done something other than beat his chest and offer a morsel of meat. Yet the discussion suggests that the additional value provided by human activity is superficial. What we *really* are is the chest-thumping

Justice and Power

ape; what sonnets and symphonies provide is just packaging. In the relationship between nature and culture, it's nature who's boss.

Suppose you agree with the most militant supporters of these views: anatomy is destiny, biology is primary, and whatever joined them later is of secondary importance. Even this doesn't commit you to what primatologist Frans de Waal calls the Veneer Theory: "We are part nature, part culture, rather than a well-integrated whole. Human morality is presented as a thin crust underneath of which boil antisocial, amoral, and egoistic passions." The word *veneer* is well-chosen by de Waal to criticize a number of views that hold that all that's natural are biologically determined drives to reproduce ourselves; culture is the transparent and thin attempt to further, while glossing over, that reality.

This view has been persuasively questioned by a number of primatologists who spend their lives studying our closest kin. Frans de Waal's work is the most philosophically far-reaching. His research on a variety of apes and monkeys led him to conclude that "we are moral beings to the core." This research is important because it begins at the bottom. It shows that even if you accept the idea that culture is trivial (or anyway evolutionarily recent) and that most of what's essential to human nature is beastly, we are much better off than supposed. The emotional responses to others' suffering, which we share with apes, are building blocks of the complex structures of human morality. DeWaal and others have shown that primates have the capacity most basic to moral development: the ability to put yourself in others' shoes. The feeling of sympathy, the capacity for gratitude, the sense of justice all start right there.

Justice and Power

In Darwin's own era, discussion of human motivation was infinitely richer than in ours. No reader of Dostoevsky or Eliot will suppose that the nineteenth century was naive about what moves us, or the curious intermixture of self-interest with other motives that trails through our actions, large and small. The difference is that until quite recently human motives were considered to be *mixed*. It seemed self-evident that people are moved by the wish to behave according to certain standards as well as the wish to secure more narrow forms of well-being. "She did it because it was right" was once, by itself, an explanatory statement – though whether that was really the reason she did it was always open to question. By the late twentieth century, such statements no longer counted as explanatory, but required deconstruction revealing some form of self-interest as the real driving force. None of the thinkers who contributed to making this assumption seem natural has asked the historical question about their own premise: might that assumption itself be part of a conceptual framework constructed during the twentieth century? The supposition that any genuine explanation of human behavior must penetrate high-flown, idealistic descriptions to reach the self-interested wheels that turn us is itself a piece of ideology whose history has yet to be written.

Evolutionary psychology is not a product of the left; it began as a theory that provoked a torrent of left-wing criticism. Reinvented under another name a few years later, it now provides the default assumptions about human behavior accepted by most people regardless of political standpoint. Those assumptions are relentlessly tribalist: protecting your own is no longer a theory or a piece of advice, it's baked into your genes. The presumptions are so widespread we rarely notice them when they regularly appear in the news or the cultural media. Unlike the work of philosophers, evolutionary psychology radiates an air of hardnosed objectivity that makes speculation look like science. Thus it functions as the backbeat for a culture in which ever more worldviews take us back to Thrasymachus. If you accept the philosophical accounts of the pervasiveness of power, what's not to like about evolutionary psychology? As the science journalist Robert Wright wrote in 2004:

> This Darwinian brand of cynicism doesn't exactly fill a gaping cultural void. Already, various avante-garde academics – deconstructionist literary theorists and anthropologists, adherents of critical legal theories – are viewing human communication as "discourses of power." Already many people believe that in human affairs all (or at least much) is artifice, a self-serving manipulation of image.[38]

Experts in many fields have worked for decades to undermine the tyranny of self-interest underlying evolutionary psychology and the worldviews it supports. The model just doesn't explain much behavior of human beings (or primates, or elephants, or, according to some studies, even rats). Unfortunately, the model underlies so many views that this careful debunking often goes unnoticed. But, even without the help of science and scholarship, a little self-reflection could convince us that we do not *always* act as the reigning ideologies suggest. We care about asserting truth, not just maintaining power; we often act with regard for others, from interests that are not material interests; and our behavior is rarely guided by the impulse to reproduce as many copies of ourselves (or our images) as possible.

There is, however, a prominent exception: Donald Trump. Unlike the rest of us, he permanently exhibits the combination of motives we are told are the true forces driving human behavior. Nor does he appear to understand any other. Though he recognizes that other people, aka losers, have norms, he has no idea of how norms work, moving people to override self-interest in order to honor them. In acting on the international stage like Richard Dawkins' ruthless genes, he has attracted millions of followers, who say they admire his authenticity. With apologies to Abraham Lincoln, he functions as a license to act according to the worst devils of our nature. The baleful fascination he exerts over the many who loathe him is a result of his singularity: it's perpetually astonishing to observe a human being who behaves so differently from the rest of us. By taking the trouble to be a hypocrite, George W. Bush paid compliments to virtue. No wonder even those who wanted him jailed for war crimes feel occasional nostalgia.

Might this example function as a *reductio ad absurdum* of the self-interested power paradigm? A world in which that model was truly universal would be a world in which everyone behaved like Donald Trump.

4
Progress and Doom

It's not accidental that most of those who would have called themselves leftists a generation ago now call themselves progressives. Fear is a factor. In a world where residues of the Cold War have yet to be examined, much less discarded, 'leftist' sounds too close to 'socialist,' and 'socialist' too close to the state socialism of Eastern Europe for comfort. Fear notwithstanding, the shift to the word 'progressive' makes more sense than naming your political standpoint after the accidental seating arrangements of the 1789 French parliament. For there's no deeper difference between left and right than the idea that progress is possible. It wasn't an idea found in traditional conservative thought, which viewed history, at best, as static or circular, and, at worst, as a sad slow decline from a mythic golden age. On this view, limited improvement may be achievable, but a truly better world could only be found in the afterlife.

What's in question is not technological progress, or what Arendt called "the relentless process of more and more, of bigger and bigger."[1] To stand on the left is to stand behind the idea that people can work together to make significant improvements in the real conditions of their own and others' lives. It's an idea that's often caricatured as the idea that progress is inevitable. Many passages of Hegel and Marx do make that claim, and history has not exactly confirmed it. But to deny that progress is assured is not to deny that it's possible, if possibility depends on the free actions of human beings working together. If progress in this sense is possible, so is regress, and history has seen both. Give up the prospect of progress, and politics becomes nothing but a struggle for power.

So how did Michel Foucault become the godfather of the woke left? His style was certainly radical, but his message was as reactionary as anything Edmund Burke or Joseph de Maistre ever wrote. Indeed, Foucault's vision was gloomier than theirs. Earlier conservative thinkers were content to warn that all hell would break loose should revolutionaries contest the traditions that carry societies along, for better and worse. Here Schmitt was exemplary and explicit: since the state lost the Lord and the sovereign in the seventeenth century, history fell into permanent decline. Foucault's warnings were more insidious. You think we make progress toward practices that are kinder, more liberating, more respectful of human dignity: all goals of the left? Take a look at the history of an institution or two. What looked like steps toward progress turn out to be more sinister forms of repression. All of them are ways in which the state extends its domination over our lives. Once you've seen how every step forward becomes a more subtle and powerful step toward total subjection, you're likely to conclude that progress is illusory. How far Foucault

Progress and Doom

believed this himself is an open question, but it's certainly the view most have drawn from his work.

If you want to take down hopes for progress, it's a stroke of genius to target one of the Enlightenment's first and most successful demands: the abolition of torture. Like most progressive demands, it was never fully realized. George W. Bush brought torture back to Guantanamo, and it is used more or less openly in much of the world today. If progress through the joint efforts of committed people is possible, so is regress. Still, standard practices like drawing-and-quartering, breaking on the rack, and *autos-da-fé* have been banned as barbaric. To appreciate how revolutionary that ban was you must know that though Voltaire and Diderot were outraged by many features of their judicial system, it took them time to get angry over torture. It was such a fixed feature of crime and punishment that they needed slow convincing. A world where radical reformers like Diderot and Voltaire were not sure whether it was legitimate to break a man on a rack in a public square is not the world we live in. Executions in the U.S. are rarely contested for the reasons one might rightly contest the death penalty, but on the grounds that the prevailing method of execution by injection may cause too much pain.

Clifford Geertz called *Discipline and Punish* Foucault's most forceful work; it's certainly the one most often taught to undergraduates. It begins with a horrific description of the slow death by torture of one Robert Damiens, executed in 1757 for attempting to kill King Louis XV. The account goes on for pages, and it remains in memory when the convoluted argument that follows is forgotten. As Améry wrote, Foucault doesn't argue;

he hypnotizes. And as ancient Greek writers noted, it's easy to feel mesmerized by spectacles of violence that also repel us. Argument or not, by the time we've finished reading *Discipline and Punish*, we can easily be convinced that modern forms of incarceration are worse than a system in which six horses and an executioner's sword publicly dismember a living human body.

Worse? If it were only that simple. Foucault wasn't the first to fudge the distinction between normative and descriptive claims, but he helped to make it common practice among legions of theorists who call themselves critical. In one of his last essays, "What is Enlightenment?," Foucault describes the demand to make normative judgments as "the blackmail of the Enlightenment," the idea

> ... that one has to be 'for' or 'against' the Enlightenment. It even means precisely that one has to refuse everything that might present itself in the form of a simplistic and authoritarian alternative: you either accept the Enlightenment and remain within the tradition of its rationalism (this is considered a positive term by some and used by others, on the contrary, as a reproach); or else you criticize the Enlightenment and then try to break from its principles of rationality (which may be seen once again as good or bad). And we do not break free of this blackmail by introducing 'dialectical' nuances while seeking to determine what good and bad elements there may have been in the Enlightenment.[2]

So what, precisely, are we meant to do? The scornful scare-quotes around the words 'for' and 'against' suggest we should be ashamed to raise such a vulgar concern. You may look for an argument; what you'll

Progress and Doom

find is contempt. Foucault makes us feel that judging something as better or worse is intellectually crude. Only simple minds ask banal questions; sophisticated thinkers gave them up long ago. So, Foucault never actually claims that bringing back drawing-and-quartering would be *better,* though he does say that the object of eighteenth-century prison reform was not to punish less but to punish better. "From being an art of unbearable sensations punishment has become an economy of suspended rights." What conclusion should the reader draw?

Nor does he hint toward any proposal that might make the lives of murderers, or people with severe mental illness, better in any way. When pushed for a solution, Foucauldians reply that their business is archaeology, a form of history, a field notoriously averse to making normative claims. Yet his vision of history is full of normative implications. Unlike those of conservatives, Foucault's histories do not begin with a golden age from which we steadily decline. There are simply brutal forms of subjugation which are replaced by more refined ones.

> Humanity does not gradually progress from combat to combat until it arrives at universal reciprocity, where the rule of law finally replaces warfare; humanity installs each of its violences in a system of rules and those proceed from domination to domination.[3]

After reading even a little of this, it's hard to avoid concluding that any attempt to improve things will only make them worse. Common-sense questions such as *would Robert Damiens have preferred incarceration in Bentham's Panopticon?* have no more room in

Foucault's thought than normative ones. Jean Améry, whose own torture at the hands of the Gestapo was considerably less gruesome than Damiens', knew what he would have chosen.

Reviewing *Discipline and Punish,* he wrote:

> Only a fool would deny that prison improvements of the 18th and 19th century were *also* an expression of bourgeois capitalist striving for profit, as if the powers that were didn't *also* consider that a halfway humanely treated prisoner has better working potential than one who is starving. But it is an aberration to describe things as if this humanization were *only* the result of profit and production.[4]

Améry reflects the sort of everyday wisdom we expect grownups to have. Whether you're thinking of reasons or causes, most events have more than one. It's particularly true in cases of progress. Consider another: American segregation was outlawed in the 1960s because many Americans, not least members of the Kennedy administration, were morally outraged by the sight of white policemen attacking black children with dogs and firehoses. When beginning the reforms later cemented by the Johnson administration, the Kennedys also knew the Soviet Union was watching the same television, and using it to attack American claims to serve as a beacon of freedom. Without the prodding provided by the Cold War, segregation would likely have lasted even longer. Knowing this may temper our admiration for the Kennedy brothers' moral outrage, but it shouldn't undermine it entirely. There is enough historical evidence to show it was real. And even were it not: how much does it matter what moved them to act? A world where all citizens have equal rights to eat, ride, and study where they want to is better than a world where they do not, and no amount of dialectical sophistication will convince a black Southerner who lived through segregation to deny it. Are you angry that those rights today are often merely formal, thwarted by roadblocks erected to prevent citizens of color from realizing them? So am I. But a world where formal rights to equal treatment exist is better than a world where we have to start legislating those rights from scratch.

Foucault doesn't care for questions of intention: if the subject itself is on the verge of disappearing, there's no need to worry about agency. Nor is he concerned with causes. Did those, like Voltaire, who fought to abolish torture really care about human suffering and human dignity and simply fail to notice they were embarking on a venture that would undermine them? Or was the move from torture to incarceration a more conscious attempt to establish more enduring control? Foucault leaves both possibilities open because he doesn't think it matters. Whether they were naive or cynical, all reformers wound up contributing to less brutal but more effective systems of power. Prison, for Foucault, is just the tip of the iceberg: "The prisons resemble factories, schools, barracks, hospitals, which all resemble prisons."[5] All of them are ways in which, through structures that usually remain invisible, we internalize mechanisms of domination and control more subtle and sinister than anything the world before Enlightenment had to offer.

Those inclined to give Foucault the benefit of the doubt will argue that his work exposes the methods of power in order to prepare the ground for changing them. Since the reforms of the Enlightenment, power has become more subtle and anonymous, hence harder to recognize. It's easy to rebel against observable tyrants, far more difficult to deny vast anonymous structures in which we participate. As the history of censorship shows, this argument has merit: where information is clearly censored, bold people will go to great lengths to get it. Where people believe they live in societies that give them full access to information, they're more likely to drown sleepily in its excesses.

This generous reading of Foucault would bring him close to Rousseau, who also criticized early Enlightenment accounts of progress. The self-taught provincial burst on the Paris scene in 1750 with a prize-winning essay, "Discourse on the Arts and Sciences," which savaged standard liberal views of the time. Against those who assumed that arts and science paved a smooth road to progress, Rousseau argued that they often simply feed authors' vanity while disguising oppressive power structures. The arts and sciences, he wrote, "weave garlands of flowers around the chains that bind us." It's a powerful critique that Foucault might have welcomed. Unlike Foucault, however, Rousseau spent the rest of his life trying to answer the problems he raised in that first essay: *how to break those chains?* Knowing how hard the problem is, Rousseau tried several solutions. In *The Social Contract* he proposed law for "men as they are and laws as they should be"; in *Emile* he proposed education for a man as he should be under laws as they are. Nowhere did he explain how to bring the two together to create free citizens in a world without domination. But it may be the hardest question to answer, in politics or in theory: *how can the chains be broken without doing more damage than the chains themselves?* At least Rousseau tried.

Progress and Doom

This gives Rousseau's deconstruction of standard accounts of progress an entirely different tone than Foucault's. Foucault preferred (rhetorical?) questions to assertions, and was happier to suggest than to stake out a claim. His books are likelier to leave the reader the reader with a mood than a position. To quote Améry once more:

> It's very hard to speak common sense with men like Michel Foucault. One always gets the worst of it – if only because his structural visions are more *aesthetically* alluring than those of critical rationalism. But to completely deny progress and to shrug your shoulders over all reforms is misguided and – I weigh my words – in the end reactionary.[6]

Of course, Foucault was disinterested in anything so common as common sense. He was one of the thinkers for whom Améry recommended a banality cure. (The other was Adorno.) Yet the reactionary kernel Améry recognized in his thought came to fruition after Améry's own death, when Foucault examined the neoliberalism that would underpin the prevailing global order. Unlike political liberalism, neoliberalism is liberalism without humanism:

> It offered a compelling terrain upon which his practical aspiration for freedom might merge with his theoretical conviction that power is constitutive of all human relationships.[7]

The philosopher Alexander Nehamas wrote: "He was always able – indeed eager – to see the dark side of every step toward the light, to grasp the price at which every advance had to be bought." Light and shadow go together; each makes the other perceptible. That's a very old trope and, though it doesn't provide a theodicy, it works as an art form. If what's at issue is a question of what's more aesthetically alluring, you might say Foucault was drawn to darkness and leave it at that. But here aesthetics have consequences. At a roundtable discussion with Foucault, several eminent historians pointed out that *Discipline and Punish* paralyzes those who wanted to work for reforms:

> If one works with prison educators, one notes that the arrival of your book had an absolutely sterilizing or rather anesthetizing effect on them, in the sense that your logic had an implacability they could not get out of.[8]

One can only pity the poor reformer who wants to better the lives of the incarcerated. Any number of improvements would do so: more space, decent food, educational opportunities, access to books and computers, improved contact with the world outside prison, not to mention an end to the corruption that places prisoners at the mercy of guards' arbitrary will. For anyone in prison, any of these could be life-changing, but Foucault explicitly scorned simple advances like the flush toilets or longer visiting hours that French prisoners demanded.[9] Thus it's hard to imagine a prison administrator making an effort to improve those conditions after reading Foucault. Didn't he just learn that improvements made in the name of human rights only lead to more sinister forms of subjection? If the book has another message, only the initiated can understand it.

Adorno and Horkheimer's influential *Dialectic of Enlightenment* takes a similarly grim view of progress. The modern world, which they date back to Homer, seeks to liberate people from the chains of tradition, but soon leads us to bind ourselves like Odysseus at the mast. I've discussed their argument at length elsewhere[10] and mention it here just to acknowledge that *Dialectic of Enlightenment*'s defenders make similar claims as did those who wanted to defend *Discipline and Punish*. Both, they argue, are not wholesale attacks on the Enlightenment. Like Foucault, Adorno and Horkheimer wished to reveal its unintended effects; after these were uncovered, the ground could be cleared for a new Enlightenment without the defects. There are passages in both books which gesture in that direction, but make no effort to point a way forward. It would be foolish to demand that philosophy provide answers to all the questions it poses. But if it doesn't provide a taste of what Kant called orientation in thinking, what good does it do?

Though Rousseau's critique of thoughtless modern assumptions about progress is fairly well known, it's common to think that other Enlightenment thinkers were blithely optimistic about the future. (Indeed, Rousseau's critique of optimism is one reason many scholars don't associate him with the Enlightenment at all – in contrast to Rousseau's most famous admirer, Immanuel Kant.) You needn't read Kant's own rather gloomy musings on the subject to be convinced that the Enlightenment was hardly as sunny as generally supposed. *Candide*, the short novel written by Rousseau's arch-rival Voltaire, will serve even better. The novel's subtitle is *On Optimism*, and its goal is to show you that optimism is ridiculous. The view is held by the foolish Dr. Pangloss, who has taught his pupil Candide that all's for the best in this best of all possible worlds.

Progress and Doom

Candide clings to the view as he journeys through a category of mid-eighteenth-century horrors, all of which actually happened: the brutal and senseless Seven Years' War, the Lisbon earthquake and the auto-da-fé which followed it, the multiple rapes of women, the execution of officers who lost battles. A voyage to the New World brings no respite from the Old, for it lays bare the evils of slavery and colonialism. Education is humbug, and none of the other engines of progress works: wealth and high culture end in boredom and gloom. This is *Candide*'s message, and if its naive hero has learned anything by the end of the story, it's to renounce his early optimism.

The belief that the Enlightenment thought progress inevitable has about the same basis as the belief that the Enlightenment was fundamentally Eurocentric, namely: none. More exactly, with few exceptions, Enlightenment thinkers' views of progress were the very opposite of the views ascribed to them today. Over and over they proclaim that progress is (just barely) *possible*; their passionate engagement with the evils of their day precludes any belief that progress is assured. Still they never stopped working toward it.

What explains the persistence of the caricature? Straw men are easy to vanquish, and those who would convince us that progress is impossible often argue as if the only alternative is the view that progress is inexorable. If the only choice is between nihilism and absurdity, most of us will reject the absurd. But I think the caricatures have deeper grounds. For all his attention to the savagery the world can offer, Voltaire didn't think human nature was fundamentally corrupt. "Man is not born evil; he becomes evil, as he becomes sick," he wrote in the

Philosophical Dictionary. Those who say we're inherently ill are sick physicians hiding the fact that they can't cure anything themselves. Voltaire's sick physicians are priests, since his goal was not to defend a utopian view that we are all naturally good, but to attack a Christian view that we are all naturally evil. Without understanding the religious context of Enlightenment views of human nature, we cannot understand them at all. They lived in a world whose institutions were grounded on the doctrine of original sin. Church views about sin varied in severity. For Calvinists, our sin is so great and God's power so vast that He can condemn any of us to eternal damnation before we've done anything to suggest we deserve it. Catholics could be saved by rituals of penance, often accompanied by bribes to those dispensing absolution. But whether redemption was ultimately possible or not, it could only come in the arms of the church, as change could only come through the hand of God. The effects of such a worldview cannot be underestimated. One didn't need to wait for the gates of hell to be assured of it: "Abandon all hope" described much life on earth.

Moral progress is only possible if human nature is better than the church taught. By urging that it wasn't, and that social conditions were natural facts, church and state sent the message that progress is impossible. It's a good way to discourage people from attempting to make any. Thus it was crucial that the Enlightenment attack Christian views of original sin. They did not do so naively. Voltaire once quipped that it was the only theological doctrine supported by evidence. Rousseau enraged his contemporaries by claiming they were much worse than they imagined. He is generally believed to have argued that human beings are fundamentally good, but he did no such thing. He thought rather that we, like other animals, are born with two inclinations: a desire for freedom and compassion for others' pain. Both inclinations can be destroyed by the wrong kind of education and social structures. Given the right conditions, they form the basis of decent behavior.

His hopes for the possibility of progress rested on a fundamental insight: "*We do not know* what our nature permits us to be."[11] In order to say that where you stand is better than where you stood you must be able to determine the latter. It would be easy to say (or deny) that human beings can make moral progress if we could trace human nature back to an original state that would allow us to measure whether we were declining or improving. That's why so many philosophers, anthropologists and biologists have speculated so often about the state of nature. Rousseau recognized early what critics of evolutionary psychology lately argue: we have no access to humankind's earliest states. Archaeology and palaeontology give us clues Rousseau never had, but they will never be enough to dismiss his deepest insight: in questions concerning the nature of human nature, we are hopelessly partisan. All the data are filtered through our own hopes and fears. Rousseau's vision of the state of nature makes warfare seem perverse; that of Hobbes makes it seem normal. If you want to establish a dictatorship, your best chance is to convince your fellows that humankind is naturally brutal and needs a strong leader to prevent it from tearing itself to bits. If you want to establish a social democracy, you will magnify every instance of natural cooperation you can find. Even while journeying to the Amazon in the hope of finding

Progress and Doom

tribes who resembled the inhabitants of Rousseau's state of nature, Claude Lévi-Strauss, the most sophisticated anthropologist who tried to test the philosopher's theses, knew that empirical methods wouldn't decide them.

This is not to say or to suggest that human nature is entirely constructed; it is to doubt that any method could determine which parts are constructed and which are not. In his typically brazen prose, Rousseau declared: "Let us begin by setting aside the facts, for they do not affect the matter at hand."[12] Since the facts are not accessible, he proposed radical honesty. Instead of making up stories designed to serve a particular worldview as the truth about human nature, why not lay your cards on the table? Not certainty but plausibility should be the test for accepting a story, if it supports a view you have other grounds to defend. We can never know what the state of nature was really like, and we ought to stop trying. Rather, the idea of the state of nature is a tool that can be used to think about the most fruitful ways of going forward.

As Kant extended the argument, we cannot act morally without hope.[13] To be clear: hope is not optimism. Optimism (and pessimism) make predictions about a distant future and an inaccessible past. Hope makes no forecasts at all. Optimism is a refusal to face facts. Hope aims to change them. When the world is really in peril, optimism is obscene. Yet one thing can be predicted with absolute certainty: if we succumb to the seduction of pessimism, the world as we know it is lost. In an era when the threats to that world seem overwhelming, pessimism is alluring, for it assures us there's nothing to be done. Once we know it is futile, we can all stop struggling. For solace, or at least distraction, there's always self-care or consumption or mind-altering substances.

Whether you see the proverbial glass as half-full or half-empty is more than a matter of temperament. If you cannot see it as half-full, you'll eventually stop trying to fill it. Maybe there was a crack at the bottom making all your efforts in vain. Following Rousseau, Kant, and Noam Chomsky, I've suggested that hope is not an epistemological but a moral standpoint. Many philosophers have taken the opposite view. The Stoics advised us to limit hope and desire if we want true contentment. In a more dramatic key, Nietzsche wrote that hope was the worst of all the evils in Pandora's box, for it ensures we will be eternally tormented. If all you seek is your own peace of mind they are probably right. And if that's the case, no philosopher can convince you otherwise. To care about the fate of the world you must love at least a piece of it. One person, perhaps even a landscape, might be enough.

Progressive would be the right name for those who lean left today, if they didn't embrace philosophies that undermine hope for progress. The man who thought original sin the basis of any sound political theory may have seen salvation in the church – at least for his friends. Schmitt's categories of political history are not only childish, as Adorno noted. Viewing politics through the lens of the friend/enemy distinction takes us back to prehistory. For Foucault, every attempt to make progress entangles us in a web that subverts it. And in convincing us that all our actions reflect our primitive ancestors' attempts to reproduce themselves, evolutionary psychology assures us that we will never

Progress and Doom

really escape from the Stone Age. Most who take evolutionary psychology for granted today know nothing of the political controversies that once surrounded it: they weren't even born when Wilson, Gould, Lewontin and others were slugging it out in Harvard Yard and the pages of the *New York Review of Books*. But despite all the criticism, evolutionary psychology has metastasized to be treated as canonical science, regardless of political leanings.

You may argue that theory is secondary: of course woke activists seek solidarity, justice, and progress. Their struggles against discrimination are animated by those ideas. But they fail to see that the theories they embrace subvert their own goals. Without universalism there *is* no argument against racism, merely a bunch of tribes jockeying for power. And if that's what political history comes to, there's no way to maintain a robust idea of justice. But without commitments to increasing universal justice, we cannot coherently strive for progress.

Most woke activists reject universalism, and stand by discourses of power, but they're unlikely to deny they seek progress. It would be easier to believe them if they were willing to acknowledge what some forms of progress had achieved in the past. Showing how each previous step forward led to two twisted steps back can be intellectually dazzling. There are enough instances of injustice to unmask so that several lifetimes won't suffice to do it. But without hope for putting something else in its place, such unmasking becomes an empty exercise in showing your savvy. You won't get fooled again.

I have spent time debunking standard contemporary readings of Enlightenment philosophers in the hope of

Progress and Doom

convincing today's progressives to reconsider them, for they provide much stronger conceptions of progress, justice, and solidarity than those which are dominant today. If we continue to misconstrue the Enlightenment, we can hardly appeal to its resources. Were I asked to attend to the principles of a racist, sexist movement that believed in inevitable progress, I'd surely change the channel. Overturning false cliches clears the ground for reviewing Enlightenment ideas and, with some revisions, putting them to work.

Yet one young journalist who was kind enough to read this book in manuscript raised a question that may occur to others. You've convinced me, she wrote, to give the Enlightenment a chance, and it's interesting to learn that Diderot wrote texts that sound like Fanon. But if Fanon is Diderot without the baggage, why can't we just read Fanon? There are many answers to the question, the first being that Fanon, who died at thirty-six, didn't have the time to expand the work he created. That work is as important as it is limited in scope. Reading Enlightenment thinkers is one way to broaden thoughts of Fanon and others to questions of first principles. Fanon was a universalist who sought justice and believed in the possibility of progress, all necessary conditions of belonging to the left. But it's important not only to apply those principles but to show how they're related and grounded, and to defend them against others which appear to have the same ends in mind.

A more general answer to the question was given by C.S. Lewis, who insisted that we should always read, at a minimum, one old book for every three new ones. Here is his argument:

Progress and Doom

> Nothing strikes me more when I read the controversies of past ages than the fact that both sides were usually assuming without question a good deal which we should now absolutely deny ... The only palliative is to keep the clean sea breeze of the centuries blowing through our minds, and this can be done only by reading old books. Not, of course, that there is any magic about the past. People were no cleverer then than they are now, they made as many mistakes as we. But not the same mistakes. Two heads are better than one, not because either is infallible, but because they are unlikely to go wrong in the same direction. To be sure, the books of the future would be just as good a corrective, but unfortunately we cannot get at them.[14]

The concept of progress is normatively tinged, one reason why those uneasy with the normative are suspicious of progress in the first place. Here Philip Kitcher's pragmatic conception of progress is helpful. It's a matter of changing direction: rather than thinking of progress as directed *to* a particular goal it can be useful to think of progress *from* a problematic situation to one that is less constrained. Progress toward universalism is as vague as it is daunting. Progress from all the conditions that stand in the way of that goal, moving from chattel slavery to segregation to systemic racism, for example, holds out more promise.[15]

But this, after all, is philosophers' talk. There's a perfectly simple reason to question the possibility of even enough progress to save the world as we know it. While I sit at a desk with a lovely view, I know the planet is alternately flooding and burning. Anyone with even a glancing interest in the news can watch disaster unrolling, and those who might prevent it sit on their hands.

Progress and Doom

Political violence is soaring, and none of the traditional mechanisms that once restrained it seem to work. The lies that stood behind institutions we once trusted now stand exposed. New plagues emerge before the old ones subside. The four horsemen of the apocalypse haunt even atheist nightmares. Who could hope for progress at a moment like this?

I have argued that hope for progress is never a matter of evidence. Nothing would be easier than to join the pessimist chorus if I thought the question could be settled empirically. It cannot. But sometimes evidence helps sustain our hope in moments when it threatens to falter. Let's return to the abolition of public torture. Banning it required not just changing opinion but changing sensibilities. You may shudder to read Foucault's description of Damiens' death (though it will likely be the passage that remains in memory long after reading). Had you been a parent in 1757, you'd have thought no more of taking your children to watch it than you'd think of taking them to the circus today. Had you been able to afford it, you'd have paid money for good seats. Versions of torture as entertainment have a long history; the Roman Colosseum was built to display them. It's a sign of deep and visceral progress that we shudder at the thought of offering live torture to children as a treat.

That some forms of torture persist in places like prisons, where they're largely hidden, is a scandal that must be addressed, along with the scandal that so many innocent people, in the U.S. as in China, are incarcerated at all. But those scandals could not even be addressed were we still in a world where leftists like Diderot and Voltaire were on the fence about whether torture should be abolished at all. (Please don't suggest that this means

Progress and Doom

they weren't really leftist. People can't be situated politically without reference to their place in time.) As for Foucault's charge that the aim of penal reforms was not to punish less but punish better: is there really any doubt about which form of punishment Damiens would have chosen?

The fact that racism persists into the twenty-first century is a disgrace that few who witnessed the Civil Rights Movement half a century ago would have imagined. What we also didn't imagine: a black family gracing the White House for eight years in our lifetime. There hadn't yet been a black cabinet member. Those who hoped that racism would retreat with the election of Barack Obama underestimated the depth of racism. Bernard Lafayette, a colleague of Dr. King's during the Civil Rights Movement, called Obama's presidency the second Reconstruction, so he was not surprised when it was followed by a second reaction in the person of Donald Trump.[16] Progress creates resistance in the form of backlash. As devastating, and often deadly, as the backlash to Reconstruction was, the Civil Rights Movement that eventually overturned it did not have to start by abolishing slavery. However appalling lynching and convict leasing were, there was no prospect of ending either as long as men and women could be bought and sold at auction. And, while many forms of racism remain to be dismantled today, we do not have to start by ending laws that kept black and white people from eating at the same lunch counters. Banal truths can be important as complex ones.

When I was a child, black and white children were not only forbidden to attend the same schools; we could not swim in the same lakes. When I was just a bit older,

Progress and Doom

I hung a photo of Sidney Poitier in my bedroom. At the time I was a member of a theater group; the photo, however, was less a statement about my professional aspirations than my political sentiments, a radical one in that time (1968) and place (Atlanta, Georgia). Many years later I stepped into my son's room and had a minor epiphany about progress: every poster he'd plastered on the walls showed photos of black men, but he wasn't making any statement at all. He just liked basketball.

What I want to underline is not only the fact of progress, but of visceral progress. The progress in undermining racism involved changes that may have begun with intellectual insight, cemented by law, but they pervade emotional perception: how white and black bodies interact with each other, from swimming pools to childhood idols to the interracial marriages which were illegal in many parts of America at the time when Obama's parents contracted one. A generation raised on "The Fresh Prince of Bel-Air" has no memory of a world in which "Leave it to Beaver" provided the major model of an American family. The superstardom of Beyoncé has eclipsed the sense of triumph when the Supremes became nationally successful; Motown was considered "race music" to be played on black stations. Seek your own cultural examples. Here I won't address the disparity between cultural and political power; life for Will Smith or Beyoncé is nothing like the lives of black teenagers in South Los Angeles. But to suggest that racism has hardly changed in a century dishonors the memory of those who struggled to change it.

As the right responds to the power of black culture, a similar reaction to women's achievements is also underway. The recent American restrictions on abortion are only the most blatant examples. Had I somehow failed to notice the persistence of the patriarchy, my daughters would regularly remind me. But the many ways in which sexism persists – and in parts of the world they are lethal – don't diminish the ways women's lives have been transformed in a generation. You need not look to Afghanistan to remind yourself of the difference. Most any mainstream film made a few decades ago contains enough sexist scenes to make you cringe. Sexual harassment was once so pervasive a part of the world that we didn't have a name for it. Women of my generation viewed it like the weather: we hoped for supervisors who didn't sexualize us as we hoped for sunny days, but were resigned to the squalls we could not prevent. Sexual harassment hasn't disappeared, of course, and the continuing presence of sexism in the workplace is well documented. I encounter it in softer forms in the refined realms of science and culture. Still behavior that once raised no eyebrows is increasingly condemned, and often actionable.

Women have always worked, more often in low-wage positions than in leading professions. But the number of women in positions of authority is incomparably greater than it was a generation ago and, while the wage gap still exists, it has lessened dramatically. Only a generation has passed since women who combined serious careers with families were a rarity, and men who supported them derided as wimps. These changes, like the others, were not just changes of mind. They touch our deepest private spheres, altering our most intimate assumptions about the ways men and women structure their relations. What changed in all these cases was not a particular piece of knowledge, but whole frameworks that embedded our lives. These are too deep to be overthrown in a generation, but it's hard to go further in challenging those frameworks without knowing how far we have come.

Here's another kind of progress that's been widely forgotten. During America's war on Vietnam it was common knowledge that the easiest way to avoid the draft was to pretend to be gay. This was no secret, for not until Obama's presidency could gays and lesbians openly serve in the military. I knew men against the war who moved to Canada, served jailtime, or even went to Vietnam. Not one was willing to feign being gay, even for the few minutes it took to face a draft board. All you had to do was walk in with a caricature of a gesture, avowing you couldn't wait to serve alongside those good-looking cadets, and you had a lifetime deferment. Though jokes about it were made during many a smoke-filled evening, no one wanted to face an inevitable rumor that the gay pose wasn't merely pretence. Today same-sex weddings are celebrated in conservative countries like Spain, Ireland, and the USA. Do vestiges of homophobia continue? How could they not? They've been alive for centuries. But there is a vast distance between the demands at Stonewall and a culture where no one blinks on hearing the phrase "his husband." Like other forms of diversity, the acceptance of same-sex relationships has a darker side, allowing corporations to advertise LGBT-friendly workplaces as a form of public relations while promoting the neoliberal policies that drive economic inequality. Nevertheless, equal rights for gays and lesbians is a major step forward that was unthinkable a generation ago.

Progress and Doom

A final instance of progress is even newer – so new, indeed, that it's stumbling like a toddler. Consider historical reckoning. Writing national histories and, even more, teaching them, was always central to constructing national identity. The recipe used to be simple: pick the pieces of the past you are proud of, tie them together into a narrative of progress, and view anything that doesn't belong to it as an unfortunate but minor detour. Students finish school with the feeling of belonging to the exceptional American project, or the glorious British nation, or the grand republic of France, or the eternal Russian motherland. Where history left wounds that cannot be ignored, the heroic narrative is exchanged for a narrative of victimhood. (Poles and Israelis excel at combining them.) National narratives oscillate: most countries seek heroic moments to magnify, though some will dwell on their losses. Till the late twentieth century, the one thing no national narrative emphasized was a nation's history of crime. Who could make an identity out of that?

The Germans. Starting several decades after World War II, West German activists, intellectuals, artists and church groups began to demand that Germany recognize its role as perpetrator of Nazi crimes. Outside Germany, the demand may look as superfluous as an insistence on recognizing that water is wet, but in the first decades after the war, most inside West Germany sounded like devotees of the Confederate Lost Cause. Few foreigners know how fondly they nursed a litany of grievance and suffering. Carl Schmitt was one of the few who said it openly, but he spoke for most of the Federal Republic: Germany was the very worst victim of the war. It took forty years for a West German president to declare that while Germans had suffered during and after the war, other peoples had suffered more, and their suffering was Germany's fault. (East Germany's self-image was very different.)[17] In the decades that followed, the idea that Nazi crimes are fundamental to German identity has solidified. Some Germans even refer to their country as "the perpetrator-nation."

No country before ever changed its self-image from hero to victim to perpetrator. Some will say no other country needed to do so: Nazi Germany's crimes were worse than any in human history. There is no scale that allows us to weigh and compare evils. But even those who argue that the Holocaust stands alone in atrocity now admit that the plunder and murder of slavery and colonialism were evils as well.

In 2019 I published *Learning from the Germans: Race and the Memory of Evil*. It argued that other nations could learn from German efforts to face up to the history no native wants to see. Nothing about the German historical reckoning was exemplary except the fact that no other country had ever done it: it was incomplete and imperfect, and only time will tell if the mistakes it made along the way can be corrected. It nevertheless opened a direction toward truth. It also showed that telling the truth about a nation's foul history need not lead to national disintegration.

When that book was published, the monument to Robert E. Lee still stood in Charlottesville, and the Confederate flag was emblazoned on the state flag of Mississippi. On two different British television programs, interviewers asked what the devil this had to do with Britain: after all, "the Germans wanted world domination." I had just time to remind them that the sun never set on the British empire before the next guest came on set. Disconsolate readers who approved the message asked if America or Britain had the conditions for historical reckoning that had been present in Germany, a nation occupied by armies that defeated it. The last time any part of the U.S. was occupied by victorious armies was when Federal troops ended Reconstruction by leaving the South in 1877; the last time England was occupied was 1066.

This objection supposes that German historical reckoning was forced, or at least facilitated, by the occupying armies. It was not. Germans viewed Allied denazification programs with contemptuous humor, part of a package of what they called victors' justice. No less savvy political observers than Albert Einstein and Hannah Arendt had no hope that Germany would ever acknowledge its guilt. Knowing how hard it was to win that acknowledgment, I hoped that America, perhaps even Britain, might be willing to face the parts of their pasts they would rather forget. Eventually. I hardly expected the tidal wave of reckoning that Black Lives Matter jump-started in the wake of George Floyd's murder in 2020.

I welcomed that wave, and still believe it's a sign of progress. Repression of national trauma is like a repression of any other trauma: it allows deep wounds to fester till they infect the rest of the body, or the body politic, contaminating the present with unexamined pasts. The fact that America is confronting slavery, and Britain colonialism, is a step forward toward healthier nations. Fierce backlash to those attempts should not surprise us. Fifty years after World War II, German efforts to reckon with Wehrmacht crimes were met with violent resistance, including mass demonstrations and firebombings.[18]

For like other forms of progress, historical reckoning doesn't proceed in straight lines. In addition to right-wing backlash, the past few years have seen some reckoning gone awry. Former British Museum director Neil MacGregor wrote that "The British use their history to comfort themselves. The Germans use their history to think about the future."[19] It's a fine form of praise but, as German reckoning becomes ossified, it's increasingly less true. An excess of focus on the past can make it difficult to see the present, much less the future. In Germany's case, fixture on one piece of the past, German antisemitism, has become so zealous that it blocks the view of the present. In particular, it diverts attention from racism toward other minorities, particularly Muslims, though some of that racism has been lethal.

There are signs that American focus on its historical crimes is moving in similar directions. By focusing too much on one sort of crime we risk losing sight of others. America is in the middle of a racial reckoning, but there's been little in the way of a broader political reckoning. One black artist I met on a panel discussion said it had never occurred to him that people could be persecuted for their politics. Many who can reel off sites of once-forgotten racial crimes have no idea how deeply most American historical narratives suppressed the memory of the political terror which, from 1946 to 1959 and beyond, destroyed a vibrant, interracial, socialist movement in the name of anticommunism.[20] W.E.B. Dubois is remembered as the great black intellectual he was; but, as in the case of his friend Albert

Einstein, the great socialist intellectual has been quietly quarantined. Those who have internalized the view that communism and fascism are identical cannot countenance the thought of tarnishing their heroes. Yet we cannot understand America or Britain's place in the world, or their possibilities for the future, until we examine not just our racial but our political histories.

In addition to warning that racial reckoning is not all there is to historical reckoning, I'm concerned about the ways in which history has become treated solely as the history of crimes and misfortunes. The burgeoning academic discipline called "Memory Studies" is almost entirely dedicated to bad memories. While we earlier neglected to honor history's victims, we are now in danger of forgetting her heroes. Yet nations need heroes. This is the only truth embedded in the ferocious backlash that has led American school boards to claim that national unity will be threatened if students read Martin Luther King or Toni Morrison.

Now every American should be proud to belong to a nation that brought forth King and Morrison, so they surely belong in any heroic pantheon. It's the general point that's important: no nation can thrive on a diet of bad memories. Most nations are born in blood, and do what they can to cover their tracks. It's hard to find one that never went sour, and violent, in the search for treasure and glory. Yet in every nation, brave people stood up against injustice, often at great cost. The U.S. is only exceptional because it was born in blood and paradox. Unlike nations founded when one tribe stopped wandering and decided to settle on some piece of ground, the U.S. came to life in a fanfare of ideals it betrayed in the moment of its founding. But

Progress and Doom

if American history is rooted in conquest and bondage, it's also rooted in resistance to conquest and bondage. That resistance should never be forgotten. Heroes remind us that the ideals we cherish were actually lived by brave human beings. By showing us justice embodied, they show us that ideals of justice are not empty phrases, and inspire us to act on them ourselves. For the history wars are not about heritage but about values. They are not arguments about who we were but who we want to be. Current debates over monuments focus attention on the question of whose statue should fall, but we need to think about the question of who should replace them.

Those debates should continue with nuance and care. I welcomed the demise of monuments to Confederate generals and the generic Johnny Rebs which adorn the central squares of Southern towns. I shuddered as some called for the demise of monuments to Abraham Lincoln. Unlike those who were calling, Lincoln gave his *life* to defend African American civil rights. (Like most Southerners, John Wilkes Booth hated Lincoln, but it was Lincoln's support for black voting rights that led him to murder.) Was Lincoln antiracist in our sense? How could he have been? Like all of us, it took time for him to free himself from the prejudice into which he was born. Were we less suspicious of progress, we could celebrate the fact that we've come further than Lincoln, while being grateful that he made such a start.

While researching *Learning from the Germans* I spent half a year in the Deep South studying early attempts at American racial reckoning. I was privileged to interview Bryan Stevenson, who was then in the process of completing the National Memorial for Peace and Justice in

Alabama, informally known as the Lynching Memorial. One of his thoughts struck me hardest:

> There were white Southerners who argued in the 1850s that slavery was wrong. There were white Southerners in the 1920s who tried to stop lynchings, and you don't know their names. The fact that we don't know their names says everything we need to know.[21]

If those names were known and commemorated, he continued, the country could turn from shame to pride.

> We can actually claim a heritage rooted in courage, and defiance of doing what is easy, and preferring what is right. We can make that the norm we want to celebrate as our Southern history and heritage and culture. (ibid.)

Heroes close the gap between what ought to be and what is. They show that it's not only possible to use our freedom to stand against injustice, but that some people actually did so.

Along with celebrating those heroes we should be wary of claims that racism is part of American's DNA. It is surely a larger part of American history than many once acknowledged, but the biological metaphor has consequences. Something that's part of your DNA is something you were born with, like the color of your eyes or the size of your nose. How could you help being racist if it's in your DNA? The metaphor recalls Daniel Goldhagen's *Hitler's Willing Executioners*, a best-selling book that tried to explain the Holocaust by claiming that German culture was always antisemitic. In the 1990s, the book was successful in Germany, largely because it served as a form of exoneration. If Germans had always been antisemitic, how could any individual

German be accountable for it? Racists are not born, they are nurtured, as Touré Reed has argued. When well-meaning liberals claim that racism is not a historically contingent fact but an inborn flaw, they can shift the blame to individuals – usually poor white "deplorables" – rather than political systems.[22]

You need not study philosophical debates about the relations between theory and practice to know at least this: what you think is possible determines the framework in which you act. If you think it's impossible to distinguish truth from narrative, you won't bother to try. If you think it's impossible to act on anything other than self-interest, whether genetic, individual or tribal, you'll have no qualms about doing the same.

There are many things philosophy is good for; one is uncovering the assumptions behind your most cherished views and expanding your sense of possibility. "Be realistic" sounds like common sense, but hidden behind it is a metaphysics that underlies many a political position, a whole set of assumptions about what's real and what's not, what's doable and what's imaginable. You can translate the advice to be realistic quite simply: lower your expectations. When you take such advice, what assumptions are you making about reality?

For millions of people, reality changed the moment chattel slavery was abolished, women allowed to vote, gay couples accorded the rights of other citizens. If you want a glimpse of reality in places where those changes are yet to come, take a look at chattel slavery in Mauritania or India, the rights of women in Saudi Arabia or Afghanistan, the criminalizing of same-sex relations in Iran or Uganda. Ideas overturned reality for people of color, women, and members of LGBTQ communities lucky enough to live in lands where other ideas resound.

I have argued that the ideas that created those new realities were born in the Enlightenment. The world changes whenever certain ideas are established as norms. To deny the reality of progress is to deny reality – as foolish when thinking of progress as when we think of the ways we reject it. For anyone who suspects I am blind to the latter: I've written more than one book about evil. There are days when I struggle with despair.

Perhaps the problem with recognizing progress lies in the concept of progress itself. By definition, progress is not whatever we have now. It isn't something that has already been attained, but something that should be attained in the future – preferably tomorrow morning. It's hard to acknowledge the previous generation's achievements as progress, precisely because the previous generation strove to make those achievements look as normal as they always should have been. A generation that grew up without racial segregation will hardly be inclined to find its absence an achievement. They're more likely to be astonished that it ever existed. And this was the goal of those who fought to overturn it: that their children should find the idea of segregation so barbaric and ludicrous that they wonder how anyone ever accepted it. Abolishing it now seems as trivial as drawing and quartering. Can't we focus on today's problems?

For the next generation, progress must mean going further to extinguish subtler forms of injustice. That's how progress works, and anger over the slow speed of progress is probably necessary to keep us fighting for it. Looking down occasionally at the shoulders we stand on is a way of gathering strength, for if we fail

Progress and Doom

to acknowledge that real progress has been made in the past, we will never sustain the hope of making more in the future. But knowing how far we remain from a just society, the progress attained in the past will never be enough to sustain us. There are, however, many people struggling for justice today who receive far less attention than the latest authoritarian demagogues. Remembering women in Iran, landless workers in Brazil, democracy activists in Congo or Myanmar, all grappling with conditions few of us can imagine, is one source of sustenance. "They don't give up hope," says Noam Chomsky, "So we certainly can't."[23]

In an insightful passage, Mary Midgley wrote: "Moral changes are, perhaps above all, changes in the kind of thing people are ashamed of."[24] She was writing of moral changes for the better, otherwise known as progress. The simplest examples are easy to find: whatever they may say in private, few are willing to make the racist and sexist excuses for jokes in public that drew laughs until recently. The internet can serve as a cesspool only because it permits anonymous attacks. Shame has its uses: if you'd be ashamed to say in person what you've said behind your Twitter handle, so much the better for hypocrisy.

But if shame can prevent our worst impulses, embarrassment can stifle our better ones. There's more than one reason why, given two unprovable explanations of human behavior and possibility, contemporary thinkers are inclined to assume "we are a bad lot," as Steven Pinker cheerfully put it. I've surveyed several views that contribute to contemporary enthusiasm for doctrines of original sin, but I want to close with one reason that's received little attention. I suspect that our fear of emphasizing the good news stems from a primitive fear: of being mocked as naive. Economist Robert Frank described this trend throughout the behavioral sciences:

> The flint-eyed researcher fears no greater humiliation than to have called some action altruistic, only to have a more sophisticated colleague later demonstrate that it was self-serving. This fear surely helps account for the extraordinary volume of ink behavioral scientists have spent trying to unearth selfish motives for seemingly self-sacrificing acts.

But the fear of embarrassment should itself be embarrassing, the sort of thing that haunted your adolescence but ought to be left behind. How often do we behave like the emperor's subjects, too spineless to point out his naked frame?

5
In Conclusion

This is a philosophical book, though it's not only meant for philosophers. There are many good books that have tried to understand the present state of the world by analyzing economic inequality or geopolitical transitions or social and other media. No sentient being, even a philosopher, would deny the importance of those factors, but I have chosen to focus on ideas. The woke call to decolonize thinking reflects the belief that we will not survive the multiple crises we've created unless we change the way we think about them. I agree that we desperately need fundamental changes in thinking, but I've urged another direction. For, as I've argued, the woke themselves have been colonized by a row of ideologies that properly belong to the right.

The swelling rage we observe across so much of the globe is partly the result of very real conditions that seem to have little to do with ideas. But that rage reflects not just the conditions themselves. You need not be well informed about alternatives to sense that our present

In Conclusion

conditions are not necessary. Things could be otherwise. As Hannah Arendt wrote:

> Rage is by no means an automatic reaction to misery and suffering as such... Only where there is reason to suspect that conditions could be changed and are not does rage arise. Only when our sense of justice is affected do we react with rage.[1]

Arendt denies that rage over injustice is in itself irrational; in order to act reasonably, we must be moved. What moves us even more than injustice is hypocrisy: "It is the semblance of rationality, much more than the interests behind it, that provokes rage."[2]

Rage is particularly acute in America, although those who spend most of their lives there only notice the explosions: a mass shooting with a higher than usual body count, an attack on the Capitol. We adjust our lives to conditions we do not know how to change. For an American living abroad who returns for a longer visit, the level of everyday rage is a palpable shock. It begins at the airport, continues on the road, and permeates the supermarket that is twice as large as any supermarket has to be. (How many choices of laundry detergent do you need to confirm that you live in a land of unlimited possibilities?) The rage is both masked and fed by the music that blares in every restaurant to ensure you must shout at your dinner partner in order to have what counts as conversation.

Much of that rage is a reasonable response to conditions that are profoundly unreasonable, though few Americans can really imagine any others. That's because they are missing what other wealthy countries call rights: health care that pays for the drugs needed to treat

In Conclusion

diseases, sick leave that covers the duration of an illness, paid vacations and parental leave, higher education and childcare. Americans call those things benefits, granted or denied at the will of their employer – a very different concept from the concept of rights. The absence of social rights affects poorest people most: those who produce and prepare our food, deliver our packages, care for our children and elders. But even two working parents in a moderately well-off family will see their salaries eaten by the costs of education and health care, their time consumed by chauffeuring children in places without public transportation.

The sense of precarity they feel stems from real changes in the global economy, but at least as important is an economic system whose need for relentless growth in consumer spending breeds perpetual dissatisfaction. You may have a fine apartment, perhaps a home of your own, but celebrity villas pop up when you're browsing the news. Why shouldn't you aspire to have one too? As any advertising agent can tell you, corporations devote billions each year to the production of envy. (Adam Curtis's brilliant documentary *The Century of the Self*, available online, describes the psychological savvy that goes into such efforts.) Those who resist the temptation to envy will have to spend all the same. The average computer lasts four years; smartphones implode even sooner. This is not an accident. Since 1924, capitalism has depended on planned obsolescence. Back then, an international association of major electronics companies decided to reduce the life expectancy of light bulbs from 2,500 hours to 1,000 hours. The craftsperson's assumption that products should last as long as possible began to crumble. Today we expect that most everything we

In Conclusion

use will fall apart shortly after the warranty expires. It's no surprise that even relatively well-to-do people feel stabs of economic insecurity. Today you may have a warm home, enough to eat, an internet connection, even the odd vacation. Do you know how to cope if the boiler, the refrigerator, and the computer all break down at once?

And however precarious or comfortable we may be individually, few can deny the urgency of the climate crisis. Political reactions, or lack thereof, were just barely rational as long as the impact of inaction seemed far off in the future. As tundra thaws and forests burn and blocks of Greenland crash to the sea, inaction seems not just irrational but stark raving mad. The super-wealthy who handle the levers of power usually have resources to weather the worst storms. But there's not enough high ground on the planet to shield all the Davos men and their grandchildren. As rising seas and roaring fires threaten to destroy the planet, corporations continue to profit by convincing us to buy trinkets designed to self-destruct and thereby wreak more damage on earth, sea, and sky. At a time when many ten-year-olds can give you a lecture on carbon emissions, what do the masters of the universe fail to see? It is so maddening to watch that we turn away as often as we can, thereby failing to contribute to solutions ourselves.

It isn't just the absence of social rights or gun laws that makes that rage burst open so loudly in the U.S., and increasingly elsewhere. It also reflects the disparity between the realities and the myths of American exceptionalism that most Americans swallow whole, especially if they've never lived in another country. Any politician running for office will express gratitude for

In Conclusion

living in the greatest country on earth. If this happened as often in other countries we would worry about fascist tendencies. Yet on so many measures of national achievement – health, poverty, life expectancy, literacy – the U.S. stands behind other developed nations. It has also more racial violence than any country not currently enmeshed in an internal war. (And, since I am one of the 40 percent of Americans who now fear the outbreak of civil war, I have no idea whether it will have exploded by the time these words are printed.) The millions of white American demonstrators during the summer of 2020 showed that rage over the continuing murder of black citizens is not confined to one tribe. For black Americans, that rage clouds every day. The most important privilege white people have is this: we never had to give our children *the Talk* to prepare them to avoid becoming victims of police violence.

Though we hear the globe has never been better connected, even well-connected Americans can be remarkably uninformed about ordinary life in the rest of the world. In recent debates over parental leave, American media has reported that the U.S. is one of only six countries in the world that requires none at all. But it's remarkably silent, and often misinformed, about the extent of parental rights in other parts of the world. Though any starlet's baby bump may be reported in the news, I have yet to meet an American who knows that Germany grants new parents sixteen months of paid leave after every child is born. That's the case if both parents share the leave; if only one parent stays home, fourteen months of paid leave are standard. Europeans, in turn, are not well-informed about the absence of labor rights in America, largely because they are so stunned by

In Conclusion

the savagery of the social system that they don't know how to report it. When I explained to German colleagues that most Americans had no sick leave amid a global pandemic, their reaction was not merely regret. They would hardly have been more shocked if I'd said we eat babies for breakfast.

Well-educated Americans will occasionally mention Scandinavia, which they view as a utopian welfare state – a description which implies neither justice nor rights. The example reinforces the idea that only small homogenous countries can afford a system of social rights, or navigate the conflicts it might bring. Even Bernie Sanders never mentions that Germany, an increasingly diverse society with the world's fourth largest economy, has a system of social rights he has yet to envision.

If rage is most visible in America, it can erupt anywhere when social rights are eroding. A decade ago, Britons were proud of the free system of higher education which has now disappeared; the Conservative government and its Brexit are undermining the National Health Service; and a combination of inflation and austerity means many Britons may have to choose between food and heat in wintertime. You needn't be an economist to know there are resources aplenty to solve all those problems, though economists have shown it.[3] Consider how quickly a vaccine was developed when a global pandemic threatened the world economy: suddenly billions were found for research and development. Malala Yousafzai computed that the amount spent on military expenses in eight days each year would fund twelve years of education for every child on earth. *Eight days a year.* Do you know how to act on that information? Does your powerlessness make you angry?

In Conclusion

Here Foucault was surely right: the levers of power are invisible, and we don't know how to move them. (Where 'we' embraces a very large number of people. Think: Barack Obama.) In his 1979 lectures on neoliberalism, Foucault argued that power is no longer political but economic, for neoliberalism has created a new form of rationality that put the state in service of the economy. Market freedom has become the state's foundation, which is why economic growth is the first thing mentioned when judging a state's success or its failure. Did Angela Merkel know she was channeling Foucault when she called for "a democracy that conforms to markets" (*marktkonforme Demokratie*)? The alternative would be markets that conform to democratic values, but that's not what's been achieved in the decades since the bipolar world order was replaced by global neoliberalism. This is an order which is compatible with many kinds of political organization, as developments in China have shown so well.

It can't be accidental that evolutionary psychology, which posits constant competition as the natural standpoint of human action, became the leading explanation of human behavior after the end of the Cold War. Evolutionary psychology seemed to provide scientific grounding, or at least buttressing, for the neoliberalism emerging as the only economic/political theory left standing when the Berlin Wall fell. More important than particular market policies are its general assumptions about human nature. Political theorist Richard Tuck wrote that

> Though the founders of modern economics, and their followers in political science, might have supposed they were

In Conclusion

engaged in a "value-free" or "scientific" investigation, in fact they were doing moral philosophy.[4]

Or as Margaret Thatcher once said: "Economics are the method; the object is to change the soul."

Have our souls been changing? Neoliberalism starts from the premise that we are best understood as "economic man," or *Homo economicus,* "solely as a being who desires wealth, and who is capable of judging the comparative efficiency of means for obtaining that end." John Stuart Mill, the philosopher who formulated that definition, quickly added that no political economist was ever so absurd as to imagine that real human beings can be captured by it. It may have seemed absurd in the nineteenth century, but today we're no longer startled by references to human capital. Employees are managed by departments of human resources; we're blithely encouraged to develop our brand; small children earn millions by opening toys on YouTube. A Bavarian investor recently copyrighted the initials Roman soldiers put on Jesus' cross: INRI. He plans to develop a product line of T-shirts and soft drinks, and was surprised that the church hadn't got there before him. Remember Marx, whose materialist atheism never precluded a sense of reverence?[5]

Foucault argued that neoliberalism made *Homo economicus* exhaustive. What was a fictional abstraction for Mill has now obscured every other idea of human being. Classical liberal economics viewed us as consumers; we are now fundamentally entrepreneurs. Political theorist Wendy Brown explains:

> . . . neoliberalism transmogrifies every human domain and endeavor, along with humans themselves, according to a

In Conclusion

specific image of the economic. All conduct is economic conduct; all spheres of existence are framed and measured by economic terms and metrics, even when those spheres are not directly monetized. In neoliberal reason and in domains governed by it, we are only and everywhere *Homo economicus*, which itself has a historically specific form ... the normative reign of *Homo economicus* in every sphere means that there are no motivations, drives, or aspirations apart from economic ones, that there is nothing to being human apart from "mere life."[6]

For Foucault, competition has replaced exchange as the basic market principle, but he does not think competition is natural. Hence the government must intervene to encourage or restore competition. As Brown points out, this has devastating consequences:

Most importantly, equivalence is both the premise and the norm of exchange, while inequality is the premise and outcome of competition. Consequently, when the political rationality of neoliberalism is fully realized, when market principles are extended to every sphere, inequality becomes legitimate, even normative, in every sphere.[7]

But even without the artificial inequality that a system based on competition must produce, the inflation of *Homo economicus* to eclipse every other sphere of the human leads to rage that is more powerful the less we are aware of it. You needn't be a Kantian to resent being treated as a means – as we all are, every day.

The neoliberalism Foucault describes is less an economic than a moral revolution, though it masquerades as sophisticated common sense. His account is all the more impressive for the fact that the reduction of

In Conclusion

human beings to human capital had only just begun when he wrote about it. But nowhere is his refusal to take a normative stand more infuriating. The analysis of what neoliberalism has done to us is so critical and trenchant that it's hard to read without looking for a barricade to mount. Now Foucault believed that power is no longer the sort of thing one can resist on a barricade. But Foucauldians are divided about whether he believed neoliberalism should be resisted at all.[8] Some of his comments seemed to welcome it. For neoliberalism, human capital is both descriptive of who we are and normative of what we should be. (*Develop your brand.*) We will never know if Foucault agreed, but he leaves us with no tools to contest it.

In the field of behavioral economics, neoliberalism allows that human behavior often deviates from the model of *Homo economicus*. The deviations considered, however, focus on the ways in which passions and perceptual distortions fail to maximize utility as the model demands. The model is the ideal; behavioral economics emphasizes the ways in which we fall short of it. The question of whether the model falls short of us is rarely raised. We saw a similar move when evolutionary psychology recast altruism as a problem. Rather than questioning the model, it explained our failures to act as the model predicted by declaring that our kinship-detectors get tricked. (Kinship detectors? Seriously?)

Neoliberalism holds human happiness to be best served by unregulated markets producing ever-increasing amounts of goods that were developed to distract us and designed to deconstruct. If you reject this vision to argue that people are more likely to flourish when engaged in common productive activities, you're likely to be dis-

136

In Conclusion

missed as an old hippy or a closet communist – although this argument is confirmed by every serious empirical study in social psychology. Even as we have come to believe, as Thatcher famously put it, that *there is no alternative* to a world ruled by economic rationality, its irrationality is demonstrated every day. Thomas Piketty summarizes:

> When people are told that there is no credible alternative to the socioeconomic organization and class inequality that exist today, it is not surprising that they invest their hopes in defending their borders and identities instead.[9]

We seem left with a choice between two kinds of irrationality, neither of which will allow us to flourish – or even survive.

We may be well on the way to becoming *Homo economicus*, yet our daily lives occasionally show us that our selves are larger than calculation can measure. Still we're blasted with messages that make us forget. With mantras like "responsibility to our shareholders," neoliberalism found gentle moralistic tones in which to dress its conviction that nothing but profit matters. Who, after all, could object to responsibility?

The violation of language is so pervasive that even those of us who are attuned to it only notice when it becomes extreme. You can go mad if you don't, occasionally, tune it out. It's hard to remember that advertising was not always so central to politics, nor was advertising itself so extreme. I refuse to purchase the boxes of blueberries my local grocery store markets as "The berry that cares." Though I know this will have no impact on the marketing or sales figures, it saves me from seething when I open the fridge in the morning.

In Conclusion

(*Berries don't care.* BERRIES DON'T CARE.) But I cannot avoid a new brand of portable toilet now installed on the street before my apartment. It's called "Cloudlet," which was harmless enough until the company began a marketing campaign declaring "Cloudlet = Love." A cynic might detect a hidden message: *Love is for shit.* I suspect the slogan was only a matter of thoughtlessness. Protest here seems senseless. But can people who are bombarded by that sort of lunacy every day be expected to question fake news?

These are uses of language we swallow without resistance, though we pay attention to others. There's no simple way to decide when language rules matter, and when they can be ignored, though it's important to know that the Nazis used the term "language rule" to mean "lie." "Responsibility to our shareholders" is a language rule that emerged when neoliberalism elevated the pursuit of profit until the only thing that matters is quarterly returns. It's not exactly a lie, just a distortion of the truth that makes it harder to raise fundamental questions, and easier to accept the inanities of advertising.

Meanwhile, the corporations who are busy being responsible to their shareholders noticed that some of the shareholders care about other words, and have changed their language accordingly. The homeless have become unhoused, people who cannot walk are now differently abled, those who were slaves are now enslaved persons. These linguistic changes are meant to express respect toward the people they name. But an unhoused person is no better off than a homeless one; if anything, the softened language makes the condition sound less painful. Being homeless is deeper, and worse than being

In Conclusion

unhoused, and the hardness of the language reflected that. Similarly, "enslaved person" takes the edge off the condition of slavery. Though we need no reminders today, those who bought and sold men and women did *not* consider them to be persons. Sometimes language should hurt as much as the circumstances it denotes; otherwise it is false to the realities it names. Around the turn of the millennium, English speakers began substituting the word "issue" for "problem," as if problems could be resolved with a softer-sounding word.

Language is always changing, and different languages solve problems very differently. Gender-inclusive language in German and English works in opposite ways. While Liz Truss was a prime ministeress in German, Meghan Markle was an actor in English. As a native English speaker I'm loathe to accept the current German suggestion, supported by government decree, that anyone who refrains from locutions like "citizens and citizenesses" is irremediably sexist. (Writers and writeresses. Bakers and bakeresses. Ad infinitum.) My own linguistic intuitions fall the other way: if professions are gender-neutral, gendering someone's profession leaves a sexist note. It takes effort to understand that someone who was raised in a different language will have different intuitions, not only about what's grammatically right and wrong but what grammatical forms shade into political rights and wrongs. Let this stand as one example of many. There are cases where two people with similar goals, like addressing the sexism built into language, will differ on the solution. It's the sort of disagreement that each side could live with, but for the fact that the line between disagreement and harm has become hard to draw.[10]

In Conclusion

We've long known that the personal is political, but when only the personal is political, we have given up hope. Changing your pronouns may feel like radical change, but the vehemence of woke arguments about the importance of pronouns is the expression of people who fear they have little power to change anything else. I have argued we have an obligation to hope for more. The argument is simple: if we do not hope, we cannot act with conviction and vigor. And if we cannot act, all the doomsayers' predictions will come true.

The woke yearn for progress as much as I do, and many of those who reject the idea of progress get up every morning to work for social change. They do not realize how heavily they are weighed down by the theoretical views they hold; largely, I believe, because those views are framed so obscurely. It's hard work to wade through the prose but, even when you've put in the work, the claims slip away through repeated sleights of hand. Attack a normative standpoint, you are told that it's merely descriptive. Raise the alarm about Schmitt's use of the term 'enemy' or evolutionary psychology's term 'selfish,' and you're dismissed as simple-minded; *surely sophisticated theorists are not so crass as to use words as we ordinarily do?* So it's worth going back to Thrasymachus to see the cruder versions of these ideas, unadorned by misty elegance. When you do, you see a set of positions born from disappointed hopes.

Because universalism has been abused to disguise particular interests, will you give up on universalism?

Because claims of justice were sometimes veils for claims of power, will you abandon the search for justice?

Because steps toward progress sometimes had dreadful consequences, will you cease to hope for progress?

In Conclusion

The disappointments are real and sometimes devastating. But rather than facing them, theory often reads them into the structure of the universe, creating a symphony of suspicion that forms the background music of contemporary Western culture.

It would be silly to claim that everyone who's heard that music is versed in evolutionary psychology or the work of Carl Schmitt. But even those who never opened a book of philosophy swim in the ideological currents that swirl around us. As *Breitbart News* put it, "politics is downstream from culture." Ideologies flourish because people want general explanations of how their world works; if they're simple explanations, so much the better. The dominant contemporary ideologies combine to create a fraudulent universalism which reduces all the complexity of human desire to a lust for wealth and power. Claiming support from economics, philosophy, and biology, the ideology of self-interest condemns every other motive of human action as self-delusion or cynical hype. Right-wing leaders like Andrew Breitbart and Mike Czernowitz embrace such views openly, which is at least intellectually coherent. As Czernowitz explained in *The New Yorker,* "Look, I read postmodernist theory in college. If everything is a narrative, then we need alternatives to the dominant narrative." He smiled. "I don't seem like a guy who reads Lacan, do I?" In less than conscious appropriation, many of the woke have inhaled this ideology, though it's completely at odds with their own moral aims.

One warm October morning I took a break from finishing this book to meet the Indian author and activist Harsh Mander in a Berlin café. Mander's tireless

In Conclusion

nonviolent fight for the rights of marginalized peoples in his homeland has earned him a place on the Nobel Peace Prize shortlist, as well as a series of death threats. He compares the silence of most of the public over the lynching of Muslims in today's India to German indifference toward violence against Jews in the 1930s. Discovering how many convictions we held in common, he asked about my current writing. I explained that I was writing about progressive abandonment of three principles essential to the left: commitments to universalism, a hard distinction between justice and power, and the possibility of progress.

Mander agreed and suggested a fourth principle: a commitment to doubt. Marxist colleagues had often asked why he wasn't a communist, given his fierce commitment to universal social and economic rights. His answer was simple: he couldn't subscribe to any movement that required him to stop questioning. "Hinduism has enormous problems," he continued. For his efforts to stop Hindu oppression of Muslims, the Modi government has charged him with terrorism. "But it has one thing the Abrahamic religions don't: all those gods and goddesses show us the need for doubt."

Doubt, of course, was fundamental to the Enlightenment, whose thinkers would have been amused to learn they shared something with the polytheistic Hindus. Gottfried Ephraim Lessing famously said he would prefer the never-ending search for truth to truth itself. No religion can put an end to violence, as recent events in India as well as in Buddhist Myanmar have made clear. But tempering commitment to your deepest principles with doubt about their application could prevent a lot of harm. Nothing is more senseless,

In Conclusion

at this moment in history, than one progressive's dismissing another over differences about what counts as discrimination.

It's often recalled that the Nazis came to power through democratic elections, but they never won a majority until they were already in power. Had the left-wing parties been willing to form a united front, as thinkers from Einstein to Trotsky urged, the world could have been spared its worst war. The differences dividing the parties were real; even blood had been spilled. But though the Stalinist communist party couldn't see it, those differences paled next to the difference between universal leftist movements and the tribal vision of fascism.

We cannot afford a similar mistake.

Acknowledgments

This book began in April 2022 as the Ashby/Tanner Lecture at the University of Cambridge: I am grateful to my hosts at Clare College, particularly to George van Kooten and Alan Short, for the opportunity that forced me to work out thoughts that had troubled me for several years. Samuel Garrett Zeitlin was one of the commentators on the lecture, and I'm indebted to him for the important and extensive comments he later provided for the book.

This book bears the stamp of many conversations with my late friend Todd Gitlin. In September 2020, disturbed by the developments I've described here, we began meeting once a week via zoom with the intention of writing a book. This is not the book we would have written together, which was solely focused on universalism. That book would have added perspectives from sociology, Todd's field, to my own philosophical ones. Still my thinking about the promise and failures of the left owes so much to the twenty years of friendship cut

Acknowledgments

short by Todd's death. His sane, sound, and tireless voice is sorely missed.

A number of friends were kind enough to comment on versions of this book in manuscript. Heartfelt thanks go to Lorraine Daston, Wendy Doniger, Sander Gilman, Eva Illouz, Philip Kitcher, Carinne Luck, Sophie Neiman, and Ben Zachariah for their many and thoughtful suggestions, even those I didn't accept. Writing this book meant seeking forms of criticism that were clear but constructive, sharp but not cutting. Whether I have succeeded is for others to judge.

It's unlikely that I would have expanded a lecture into a book at all were it not for the chance to work once again with Ian Malcolm, who edited my *Evil in Modern Thought* twenty years ago. Ian is simply the best editor I ever met, who provided both penetrating criticism and unlimited encouragement in this book as in the earlier one.

As always, the wisdom and steady support of my agent, Sarah Chalfant, were crucial in keeping me focused and grounded.

Notes

1 Introduction
1 Thomas Piketty, *Time for Socialism: Dispatches from a World on Fire* (New Haven, CT: Yale University Press, 2021).
2 Thomas Piketty, *Capital and Ideology* (Cambridge, MA: Harvard University Press, 2020).
3 Barbara Smith, quoted in Olúfémi O. Táíwò, "Identity Politics and Elite Capture," *Boston Review*, May 7, 2020.
4 Touré Reed, *Toward Freedom: The Case Against Racial Reductionism* (London: Verso, 2020).
5 https://www.mckinsey.com, 2021.
6 *New York Times*, January 23, 2020.

2 Universalism and Tribalism
1 Kwame Anthony Appiah, *The Lies that Bind: Rethinking Identity* (New York: Liveright, 2018).
2 Benjamin Zachariah, *After the Last Post: The Lives of Indian Historiography* (Berlin, Boston: De Gruyter Oldenbourg, 2019).
3 YouTube: https://www.youtube.com/watch?v=3qkOUXkBNS4&ab_channel=RyanLong

4 See Neiman, *Heroism for an Age of Victims* (New York: Liveright, 2024), forthcoming.
5 https://edition.cnn.com/2022/03/10/us/jussie-smollett-sentencing-trial/index.html
6 Gil Ofarim. https://www.spiegel.de/panorama/justiz/gil-ofarim-muss-sich-ab-oktober-in-leipzig-vor-gericht-verantworten-a-f6996243-62d7-4fd8-af1a-c735ae8af9d0
7 Jean Améry, *At the Mind's Limits: Contemplations by a Survivor on Auschwitz and Its Realities* (Bloomington: Indiana University Press, 1980).
8 Olúfémi O. Táíwò, *Elite Capture: How the Powerful Took Over Identity Politics (And Everything Else)* (Chicago: Haymarket Books, 2022), p. 20.
9 Miranda Fricker, "Feminism in Epistemology: Pluralism without Postmodernism" in Fricker and Hornsby, eds., *The Cambridge Companion to Feminism in Philosophy* (Cambridge: Cambridge University Press, 2016), pp. 146–65. See also Fricker, *Epistemic Justice: Power and the Ethics of Knowing* (Oxford: Oxford University Press, 2007).
10 For further argument on this score see Omri Boehm, *Radikal Universalismus* (Berlin: Ullstein Verlag, 2022).
11 For a particularly nuanced argument see K. Fields and B. Fields, *Racecraft: The Soul of Inequality in American Life* (London: Verso, 2012).
12 James Q. Whitman, *Hitler's American Model: The United States and the Making of Nazi Race Law* (Princeton: Princeton University Press, 2017).
13 Jean-Paul Sartre, "Materialism and Revolution" in *Literary and Philosophical Essays* (New York: Collier Books, 1962).
14 Ato Sekyi-Otu, *Left Universalism, Africacentric Essays* (New York: Routledge, 2019).
15 Carl Schmitt, *The Concept of the Political* (Chicago: University of Chicago Press, 1996).

16 Joseph de Maistre, *Considerations on France*, ed. Richard A. Lebrun with an introduction by Isaiah Berlin (New York: Cambridge University Press, 1994).
17 See Raphael Gross, *Carl Schmitt and the Jews* (Madison: University of Wisconsin Press, 2007).
18 See Mark Lilla, *The Once and Future Liberal: After Identity Politics* (London: HarperCollins, 2017).
19 Thomas Keenan, "Or Are We Human Beings?" in *e-flux*, 2017.
20 Eleanor Roosevelt, *On the Adoption of the Universal Declaration of Human Rights*, delivered 9 December 1948 in Paris, France.
21 United Nations, Office of the High Commissioner for Human Rights, 2018.
22 Marquis de Sade, *Juliette*; see also Neiman, *Evil in Modern Thought* (Princeton: Princeton University Press, classics edn., 2015).
23 Jean-Jacques Rousseau, *First and Second Discourses Together with the Replies to Critics and the Essay on Language*, Victor Gourevitch, ed. and trans. (London: HarperCollins, 1986).
24 Denis Diderot in Sankar Muthu, *Enlightenment Against Empire* (Princeton: Princeton University Press, 2003). Anyone interested in a more detailed development of the claims I make here should read Muthu's superb book.
25 Immanuel Kant, *Toward Perpetual Peace*, Third article: "The law of world citizenship is to be united to conditions of universal hospitality." earlymoderntexts.com
26 Diderot in Muthu, op. cit.
27 Kant, *The Metaphysics of Morals* (Cambridge, Cambridge University Press, 2017).
28 Kant, in Emmanuel Chukwudi Eze, *Race and the*

Enlightenment: A Reader (Cambridge, MA: Blackwell, 1997).
29 Chukwudi Eze, ibid.
30 Jean-Paul Sartre, Introduction to Frantz Fanon, *The Wretched of the Earth* (New York: Grove Press, 2005).
31 A. Ghose, in P. Mishra, *From the Ruins of Empire: The Revolt Against the West and the Remaking of Asia* (Harmondsworth: Penguin, 2013), p. 223.
32 Ludwig Wittgenstein, *Philosophical Investigations* 4th edn. (Oxford: Wiley-Blackwell, 2009).
33 A. Cabral, quoted in Táíwò, p. 82.
34 Sekyi-Otu, op. cit., p. 6.
35 Táíwò, *Against Decolonization: Taking African Agency Seriously* (London: C. Hurst & Co., 2022), p. 6.
36 Fanon, *Black Skin, White Masks* (New York: Grove Press, 2008).
37 Sekyi-Out, op. cit., p. 169.
38 A. Cabral, *National Liberation and Culture*. In P. Williams and L. Chrisman, eds., *Colonial Discourse and Postcolonial Theory* (London: Routledge, 1994).
39 *Cabralista* (film).
40 Sekyi-Otu, op. cit, p. 14.
41 See Benjamin Zachariah, op. cit.
42 Aime Cesaire, *Letter to Maurice Thorez* (Editions Presence Africaine, 1957).

3 Justice and Power
1 Richard Rorty, *Achieving our Country: Leftist Thought in Twentieth-Century America* (Cambridge, MA: Harvard University Press, 1998).
2 Bernard Williams, *Truth and Truthfulness: An Essay in Genealogy* (Princeton: Princeton University Press, 2002).

Notes to pages 62–72

3 Michael Walzer, "The Politics of Michel Foucault," *Dissent*, 1982.
4 Michel Foucault, "Nietzsche, Genealogy and History" in *Language, Countermemory and Practice* (Ithaca, NY: Cornell University Press, 1980).
5 See Walzer, op. cit.
6 Laura Stoler, *Race and the Education of Desire: Foucault's History of Sexuality and the Colonial Order of Things* (Durham and London: Duke University Press, 1995).
7 Edward Said, *Culture and Imperialism* (New York: Vintage, 1994), p. 31.
8 Michel Foucault, "Truth and Power" in Gordon Colin, ed., *Power/Knowledge: Selected Interviews and Other Writings 1972–1977* (New York: Vintage, 1980).
9 Michel Foucault, ibid.
10 YouTube, Foucault and Noam Chomsky. https://www.youtube.com/watch?v=3wfNl2L0Gf8&t=796s&ab_channel=withDefiance
11 Michael Walzer, op. cit.
12 S. Neiman, *Moral Clarity: A Guide for Grownup Idealists* (Princeton: Princeton University Press, 2010).
13 Alan Wolfe, *The Future of Liberalism* (New York: Vintage, 2009), p. 141. See also Richard Wolin, "The Cult of Carl Schmitt" in *Liberties*, 2022.
14 Samuel G. Zeitlin, "Indirection and the Rhetoric of Tyranny: Carl Smith's *The Tyranny of Values 1960–1967*," in *Modern Intellectual History* (Cambridge: Cambridge University Press, 2021).
15 Theodor Adorno, *Minima Moralia* (Berlin: Suhrkamp, 1969).
16 Carl Schmitt, "Amnestie – Urform des Rechts," in Stuttgart: *Christ und Welt*, 1949.
17 Carl Schmitt, *The Concept of the Political* (Chicago: University of Chicago Press, 2007), pp. 27–8.

18 Carl Schmitt, *Ex Captivitate Salus: Erfahrung aus der Zeit 1945–1947* (Cambridge: Polity, 2017).
19 Carl Schmitt, *The Concept of the Political*, p. 33.
20 See Neiman, "Antimodernismus: Die Quellen allen Unglücks?" *Die Zeit*, 2016.
21 Quoted in Zeitlin, op. cit.
22 Carl Schmitt, *Die Tyrannei der Werte* (Berlin: Duncker und Humblot, 2020).
23 Against this view see Richard Wolin, *Heidegger in Ruins: Between Philosophy and Ideology* (New York: Yale University Press, 2023).
24 Erika Lorraine Milam, *Creatures of Cain: The Hunt for Human Nature in Cold War America* (Princeton: Princeton University Press, 2019), p. 274.
25 Geertz, review of Donald Symons, *The Evolution of Human Sexuality*, in *New York Review of Books*, January 24, 1980.
26 Richard Alexander, quoted in Philip Kitcher, *Vaulting Ambition: Sociology and the Quest for Human Nature* (Cambridge, MA: MIT Press, 1987), p. 274.
27 Stephen Jay Gould, *Ever Since Darwin: Reflections on Natural History.* (New York, London: W.W. Norton & Company, 1992), p. 258.
28 Kitcher, op. cit., p. 256.
29 Kitcher, op. cit., p. 435.
30 Vickers and Kitcher, "Pop Sociobiology Reborn: The Evolutionary Psychology of Sex and Violence," in C.B. Travis, ed., *Evolution, Gender and Rape* (Cambridge, MA: MIT Press, 2003), p. 2.
31 David Barash, quoted in Kitcher, op. cit.
32 Mary Midgley, *Evolution as a Religion* (London: Routledge Classics, 2002), p. 137.
33 E.O. Wilson, *On Human Nature* (London: Penguin, 1995), pp. 155–6.
34 Stephen Pinker, "The Moral Instinct" in Hilary Putnam,

Susan Neiman and Jeffrey Schloss, eds., *Understanding Moral Sentiments: Darwinian Perspectives?* (New York: Transaction Publishers, 2014), p. 69.
35 Midgley, op. cit., p. 152.
36 Kitcher, op. cit., p. 403.
37 Midgley, op. cit., p. 152.
38 Robert Wright, *The Moral Animal: Why We Are The Way We Are: The New Science of Evolutionary Psychology* (New York: Vintage, 1994).

4 Progress and Doom

1 Hannah Arendt, *On Violence* (Oxford: Harcourt, 1970), p. 82.
2 Michel Foucault, "What is Enlightenment?" in P. Rabinow, ed., *The Foucault Reader* (New York: Pantheon, 1984).
3 Michel Foucault, "Nietzsche, Geneaology, History," op cit., p. 151.
4 Jean Améry, Werke VI, p. 214.
5 Michel Foucault, *Discipline and Punish: The Birth of the Prison* (London: Penguin, 2020).
6 Jean Améry, "Michel Foucault's Vision des Kerker-Universums" in *Merkur* (Stuttgart: Klett-Cotta), April 1977.
7 Michael C. Behrent, *Liberalism without Humanism* (Cambridge: Cambridge University Press, 2009).
8 Quoted in Raymond Tallis, *Enemies of Hope: A Critique of Contemporary Pessimism* (New York: St. Martin's Press, 1999), p. 67.
9 Michel Foucault, *Language, Countermemory and Practice,* op. cit., p. 227.
10 In Neiman, *Moral Clarity* and Neiman, *Heroism in an Age of Victims.*
11 Jean-Jacques Rousseau, *Emile, or: On Education* (New York: Basic Books, 1979).

12 Jean-Jacques Rousseau, *Discourse on Inequality* in Gourevitch, ed., op. cit.
13 Immanuel Kant, *Religion Within the Limits of Reason Alone* (Cambridge: Cambridge University Press, 1998).
14 C.S. Lewis, "Introduction" in Athanasius, *On the Incarnation* (Kentucky: GLH Publishing, 2018).
15 Philip Kitcher, *Moral Progress* (Oxford: Oxford University Press, 2021).
16 Neiman, *Learning from the Germans: Race and the Memory of Evil* (New York: Farrar, Straus and Giroux, 2019).
17 Neiman, ibid., ch. 2.
18 See Hamburger Institut für Sozialforschung (HG), *Eine Ausstellung und Ihre Folgen* (Hamburger Edition, 1999).
19 Neil MacGregor, *Guardian*.
20 For a recent exception see Reed, op. cit.
21 Bryan Stevenson, interview in Neiman, *Learning from the Germans*, op. cit., ch. 8.
22 Touré, op. cit.
23 Noam Chomsky, interview with David Barsamian, in *The Nation*, October 11, 2022.
24 Midgley, op. cit., p. 170.

5 In Conclusion

1 Hannah Arendt, op. cit., p. 63.
2 Ibid., p. 66.
3 For one example see Piketty in ibid. and Piketty, *Capital in the Twenty-First Century* (Cambridge, MA: Harvard University Press, 2013).
4 Richard Tuck, "The Rise of Rational Choice" in *European Journal of Sociology* (Cambridge: Cambridge University Press, 2005), p. 587.
5 Karl Marx, *The Communist Manifesto*: "All that is solid melts into air, all that is holy is profaned."

Notes to pages 135–39

6 Wendy Brown, *Undoing the Demos: Neoliberalism's Stealth Revolution* (New York: Zone Books, 2015).
7 Ibid.
8 See Brown, op. cit., and Sawyer and Steinmetz-Jenkins, eds., *Foucault, Neoliberalism and Beyond* (London: Rowman and Littlefield, 2019).
9 Piketty, *Capital and Ideology*, op. cit.
10 This formulation was suggested by Emily Dische-Becker.